Our Spiritual Crisis

The Master Hsüan Hua Memorial Lecture series

The First Master Hsüan Hua Memorial Lecture
Rationality and Religious Experience: The Continuing Relevance of the World's Spiritual Traditions
HENRY ROSEMONT, JR.

The Second Master Hsüan Hua Memorial Lecture
Worldly Wonder: Religions Enter Their Ecological Phase
MARY EVELYN TUCKER

The Third Master Hsüan Hua Memorial Lecture is not available as a book in this series; published as "On State and Religion in China: A Brief Historical Reflection," *Religion East and West* 3 (June 2003), 1–20.

The Fourth Master Hsüan Hua Memorial Lecture
Our Spiritual Crisis: Recovering Human Wisdom in a Time of Violence
MICHAEL N. NAGLER

The Fifth Master Hsüan Hua Memorial Lecture
The Universal Grammar of Religion
HUSTON SMITH (forthcoming)

Our Spiritual Crisis

Recovering Human Wisdom in a Time of Violence

MICHAEL N. NAGLER

With a Commentary by
Lewis S. Mudge

Followed by a Response, Discussion,
and Epilogue

The Fourth Master Hsüan Hua
Memorial Lecture

OPEN COURT
Chicago and La Salle, Illinois

To order books from Open Court, call toll-free 1-800-815-2280, or visit our website at www.opencourtbooks.com.

Open Court Publishing Company is a division of Carus Publishing Company.

First printing 2005
Second printing 2006

Library of Congress Cataloging-in-Publication Data

Nagler, Michael N.
    Our spiritual crisis : recovering human wisdom in a time of violence / Michael N. Nagler ; with a commentary by Lewis S. Mudge.
        p. cm. — (The fourth Master Hsüan Hua memorial lecture)
    Includes bibliographical references and index.
    ISBN-13: 978-0-8126-9581-6 (pbk. : alk. paper)
    ISBN-10: 0-8126-9581-X (pbk. : alk. paper)
        1. Religion and culture—United States. 2. United States—Religion.
3. United States—Social conditions. 4. Nonviolence—Religious aspects.
5. Materialism. 6. Consumption (Economics) 7. Consciousness. I. Title.
II. Master Hsüan Hua memorial lecture ; 4.

    BL2525.N34 2005
    201'.7—dc22

                                       2005013756

CONTENTS

THE FOURTH HSÜAN HUA
MEMORIAL LECTURE

*T*his book is fourth in a series that presents informal discussions of the interaction between religion and the modern world. The series is based on the annual lectures given in honor of the late Venerable Master Hsüan Hua, the eminent Buddhist monk and teacher. The lectures are co-sponsored by the Institute for World Religions and the Graduate Theological Union in Berkeley, California.

Our Spiritual Crisis begins with the Ven. Hsüan Hua Memorial Lecture given in the fall of 2003 by Michael Nagler, a leading voice in nonviolence studies. In the pages that follow, Professor Nagler argues that the modern addiction to overconsumption and to violence can be broken only by a reassessment of our view of reality. He argues that we must move into a paradigm shift toward a conception of human beings and the world as fundamentally spiritual rather than material.

Professor Nagler suggests that the idea of mono-theism has from its beginnings corresponded to the idea of the sacredness of the individual, but that this sacredness has been obscured by our addiction to materialism. To facilitate this overdue paradigm shift, Professor Nagler believes, we will need to learn meditation practices, and we will need to engage in a systematic development of nonviolence.

Professor Nagler's theme is further explored and developed in Professor Lewis S. Mudge's response, in Professor Nagler's reply to that response, and in his replies to questions from members of the lecture audience.

Michael N. Nagler is the founder and former chair of the Peace and Conflict Studies Program at the University of California at Berkeley, where he recently retired from faculty positions in Classics and Comparative Literature. He is a longtime resident and workshop presenter at the Blue Mountain Center of Meditation. He has written and lectured widely on nonviolence; his latest volume, *The Search for a Nonviolent Future* (Berkeley Hills Books), received an American Book Award in 2002. A new edition appeared in 2004. His many other publications include *America Without Violence* (Island Press) and *The Upanishads* (Nilgiri Press).

Lewis S. Mudge is Robert Leighton Stuart Professor of Theology Emeritus at the San Francisco Theological Seminary and the Graduate Theological Union. His books include *The Church as Moral Community: Ecclesiology and Ethics in Ecumenical Debate* (Continuum, 1998).

A BRIEF PORTRAIT
OF THE VENERABLE MASTER
HSÜAN HUA

*T*he Venerable Master Hsüan Hua (1918–1995) was born into a peasant family in a small village on the Manchurian plain. He attended school for only two years, during which he studied the Chinese classics and committed much of them to memory. As a young teenager, he opened a free school for both children and adults. He also began one of his lifelong spiritual practices: reverential bowing. Outdoors, in all weather, he would make over eight hundred prostrations daily as a profound gesture of his respect for all that is good and sacred in the universe.

He was nineteen when his mother died, and for three years he honored her memory by sitting in meditation in a hut beside her grave. It was during this time that he made a resolve to go to America to teach the principles of wisdom. As a first step, at the end of the period of mourning, he entered San Yüan Monastery, took as his teacher Master Chang Chih, and subsequently received the full ordination of a Buddhist monk at Pu To Mountain. For ten years he devoted himself to study of the Buddhist scriptural tradition and to mastery of both the Esoteric and the Chan schools of Chinese Buddhism. He had also read and contemplated the scriptures of Christianity, Daoism, and Islam. Thus, by the age of thirty, he had already established through his own experience the four major imperatives of his later ministry in America: the primacy of the monastic tradition; the essential role of moral education; the need for Buddhists to ground themselves in traditional spiritual practice and authentic scripture; and, just as essential, the importance and the power of ecumenical respect and understanding.

In 1948, Master Hua traveled south to meet the Venerable Hsü Yün, who was then already 108 years old and China's most distinguished spiritual teacher. From him Master Hua received the patriarchal transmission in the Wei Yang lineage of the Chan school. Master Hua subsequently left China for Hong Kong. He spent a dozen years there, first in seclusion, then later as a teacher at three monasteries that he founded.

Finally, in 1962, he went to the United States, and by 1968, he had established the Buddhist Lecture Hall in a loft in San Francisco's Chinatown. There he began giving nightly lectures in Chinese to an audience of young Americans. His texts were the major scriptures of the Mahayana. In 1969, he astonished the monastic community of Taiwan by sending there for final ordination two American women and three American men, all five fully trained as novices, conversant with Buddhist scripture, and fluent in Chinese. During subsequent years, the Master trained and oversaw the ordination of hundreds of monks and nuns who came to California from every part of the world to study with him. These monastic disciples now teach in the twenty-eight temples, monasteries, and convents that the Master founded in the United States, Canada, and several Asian countries. They are also active, together with many volunteers from the laity, in the work of the Buddhist Text Translation Society, which to date has issued over 130 volumes of translation of the major Mahayana sutras and instructions in practice given by the Master.

As an educator, Master Hua was tireless. From 1968 to the mid-1980s he gave as many as a dozen lectures a week, and he traveled extensively on speaking tours. At the City of Ten Thousand Buddhas in Talmage, California, he established formal training programs for monastics and for laity; elementary and secondary schools for boys and girls; and Dharma Realm Buddhist University, together with its branch, the Institute for World Religions, in Berkeley. In forming the vision for all of these institutions, the Master stressed that moral education must be the foundation for academic learning, just as moral practice must be the basis for spiritual growth.

The Venerable Master insisted on ecumenical respect, and he delighted in interfaith dialogue. He stressed commonalities in religious traditions—above all, their emphasis on proper conduct, compassion, and wisdom. He was also a pioneer in building bridges between different Buddhist national traditions. He often brought monks from Theravada countries to California to share the duties of transmitting the precepts of ordination. He invited Catholic priests to celebrate the Mass in the Buddha Hall at the City of Ten Thousand Buddhas, and he developed a late-in-life friendship with Paul Cardinal Yü Bin, the exiled leader of the Catholic Church in China and Taiwan. He once told the cardinal: "You be a Buddhist among the Catholics, and I'll be a Catholic among Buddhists." To the Master, the essential teachings of all religions could be summed up in a single word: wisdom.

Our Spiritual Crisis

IT IS INDEED AN HONOR TO BE INVITED to present the fourth annual memorial lecture in the name of Master Hsüan Hua, whom I once met—or rather in whose presence I was briefly privileged to be—and I still feel some effects of that meeting after more than thirty years. Master Hua attained *mahasamadhi* in 1995, only a few years before my own spiritual teacher, Sri Eknath Easwaran. Surely these were great spirits who left this troubled world of ours much better off for their presence in it, and the remarks that follow are my inadequate attempt to pay them homage.

Last spring I had the privilege of listening to United States Representative Dennis Kucinich when he addressed a group of progressive entrepreneurs in upstate New York. During the interesting question-and-answer that followed his talk, someone asked him to comment on the problem of overconsumption in this country. He shot back, "That's a spiritual problem."

What he meant was that overconsumption, be it of food or of fuel, is not a problem that legislators can solve for us by passing laws. It arises from a deep spiritual emptiness that can never be filled by anything outside us, anything that we try to consume. But Representative Kucinich's answer goes deeper than that, into the heart of many problems we are facing today, perhaps to the entire *problématique* of our modern industrial civilization.

The moment I heard Representative Kucinich's observation I was taken back to the evening of September 20, 2001, when Rabbi Michael Lerner spoke to an overflow audience in Wheeler Hall for a post-9/11 teach-in sponsored by the students in my Peace and Conflict Studies Program at the University of California at Berkeley. The burden of his talk was simply, and starkly, that we are passing through a spiritual crisis; and he electrified the audience. We knew he did not mean that the 9/11 disaster had precipitated a spiritual crisis, but that it was a result of it; and that if we do not find a way to resolve this crisis, it will not be the last such symptom. I believe he was exactly correct. The fact is that America as a whole has not found a way to respond to the tragedy of 9/11 in terms of its real meaning. This is a failure which may threaten our existence as a nation, as it has already begun to compromise our meaning as a democracy.

It is this crisis which led up to the disaster of 9/11—for example—by creating in the industrial world an artificial dependence on the resources of others. We have done nothing since 9/11 but perpetuate the crisis—for example, by drawing a curtain over the all-important question of what caused this attack upon us and by contenting ourselves with a reflexive response of vengeance.

I propose, then, to step back and ask three very large questions. What is a spiritual crisis? What is the nature of this one in particular? And what can we do about it? Bold questions, but I do not believe we can avoid them. As Martin Luther King Jr. once said, "Our lives begin to end the day that we remain silent over things that matter." In the case of the last (and most important) question, the pragmatic one, we should not expect an easy answer, and I cannot furnish one; but I do believe we can frame our understanding of the first two questions in a way that can help guide us toward the third.

QUESTION ONE

My spiritual teacher, Sri Eknath Easwaran, grew up in Kerala, on the southwest coast of India. In describing our times he used a very simple analogy, drawn, as usual with him, from his personal experience. When he was a boy in Kerala, walking along the rice paddies at a certain time of year, he would come across the abandoned skins of snakes, which are such an abundant and not always appreciated part of India's wildlife. He would ask *his* spiritual teacher, his grandmother, what they were; and she would tell him, "Son, those are the old, worn-out skins of snakes that live nearby." He would ask, "Doesn't it hurt when they shed their skin?" And she would reply, "It does. But the snakes have outgrown those skins, and if they don't shed them when the time comes, they will die."

A spiritual crisis occurs when a people (a civilization or a culture) finds itself trapped in an outmoded, suffocating network of values and conceptions, in a worldview, a "creed outworn," that has become too small to allow the people to get on with their cultural evolution. If that people does not shed its constricting vision—a process that we cannot expect to be without pain and struggle—it will die, culturally and perhaps literally as well. My fear is that today, as 9/11 shows, we may die as literally as those cobras and anacondas would have in the Kerala rice paddies. Such is the potential for chaos and violent upheaval in the present crisis, and it grows greater the longer we put off its conscious resolution.

A spiritual crisis, then, is a kind of paradigm shift in a distressing phase, when the old paradigm is becoming obviously unworkable but the new one has not yet, at least for most people, appeared over the horizon to replace it. Although it doubtless follows the dynamic of paradigm shifts structurally, a spiritual paradigm shift is special in that it involves a large element of faith, of normative outlook, of vision. We could perhaps have gone on believing that the world was flat (or even that everything revolves around the Earth) for some decades longer than we did; but I doubt we can survive much longer believing that we are separate, material objects rucking around aimlessly in a random universe.

QUESTION TWO

I have thus already suggested what I, like many, consider to be the nature of *our* spiritual crisis. As a visitor to this country recently noted, "I have never seen a country with so much religion, and I have never seen a country with so little spirituality."[1] When the recently beatified Mother Teresa said that here in America we have the "spiritually poorest of the poor," she was making the same point. What does this mean, exactly? The Scottish Council of Churches has defined spirituality as "an attempt to grow in sensitivity to self, to others, to nonhuman creations and to God who is within and beyond this totality."[2] This is to me a perfect definition of spirituality, and it throws into immediate relief the crisis that we are passing through, for it is obvious that people today have a severe hunger for contact with the spiritual, with the spiritual side of their own nature (and with nature at large). For the modern world, however, it may be necessary to enlarge this definition and try to do so in a way that avoids what a Quaker friend of mine calls "the God language."

It was my friend Willis Harman who first brought home to me the simple truth that we are living with a worldview which sees the fundamental reality of all that exists as *matter*. What is trying to happen right now is a shift to a vision in which everything is based instead on *consciousness*. This is profound and helpful, and I would like to expand on it.

Most of us would probably agree that the universe seems to consist of three ontological realms—matter, energy, and consciousness—corresponding to the traditional hierarchy of body, mind, and spirit within the human microcosm. In the view that came to be called the "prevailing paradigm" when we began rethinking it in the 1970s, matter is ultimately real and is the underlying reality of everything else. There is also energy, widely supposed to be matter in another form (as Einstein's formula was interpreted, informally, in this view); and from matter-energy there arises, inexplicably, what is called the "emergent property" of consciousness, an unexplained epiphenomenon in this still-prevalent view. Any newspaper will tell you in solemn scientific rhetoric and with numbers to prove it that you like peanut butter because of your genes and are attracted to your partner because of his or her pheromones. Today many of us cannot help regarding this orthodoxy, which Huston Smith so rightly has called "scientism"—the belief that the facts available to normal science are the only reality—as a particularly unfortunate form of arrogance.

Note that real scientists are not saying any such thing. The headline to a recent example of such claims from my local paper reads, "Study: Molecule Behind Nicotine Addiction."[3] The subhead, however, already begins to back away from this bald (and patently false) assertion: ". . . CA Researchers say reaction *partly* to blame for smokers' craving" (my emphasis). And if one were to look objectively at what the data actually say, they would say that there is a *correlation* between the molecular and the experienced, consciousness-reality—that and nothing more. It is our paradigm that for better or worse decides which comes first (assuming that one causes the other at all). It is interesting to note the subtle shifts by which, as we pass through progressive "filters," the neutral truths of science are vetted to present an extreme and unrelenting bias to the unsophisticated public: we are bodies, not spirit; helpless pawns, not moral agents. This is particularly ironic now that science—thanks in part to more sophisticated noninvasive technologies for observing changes in the living nervous system and in part to the very struggle we are describing, the struggle of the new paradigm to break out of this dismal materialism—is weighing in with more and more evidence for the primacy of consciousness and the "inter-being" of all sentient existence.[4] It is not that this is a brand new development. "Consciousness I regard as fundamental. I regard matter as derivative from consciousness . . . everything that we regard as existing postulates consciousness," said Max Planck at the beginning of the quantum revolution. How prophetic—and yet how inaccessible, still, to the general public. And for this most of the blame goes to their media—the culture that their media create and sustain.

Let me spell out, in the light of Planck's insight, what I take to be the fundamental structure of this still-uncompleted paradigm shift. From "our," already shifted, side, the system of thought that posits a matter → energy → consciousness (M-E-C) universe is exactly wrong. The universe is decidedly consciousness → energy → matter, C-E-M. The entire wisdom tradition (to use a helpful term, which I think we also owe to Huston Smith) states, to quote the Upanishads, "Prajñānam brahmaḥ" (Brahman [the ultimate Reality] is consciousness). Moreover, the wisdom tradition even has something like an explanation for the age-old dilemma: how can something that exists in space-time, like the body, interact with an element like consciousness, which does not? How does matter-energy precipitate, as it were, out of pure consciousness? Well, it actually doesn't, really, is the eternal explanation. Instead, matter-energy, name-and-form, consists of *appearance*. "Alles vergängliche ist nur ein Gleichniss," declares Goethe unequivocally at the end of *Faust*: "Everything that passes [and what in the phenomenal world does not?] is mere appearance"—a.k.a. *māyā*.

Many of us have long felt that this paradigm shift has, or would have if we could only get it to happen, profound consequences for how we live our daily lives. It could, in the terms of this present discussion, resolve the spiritual crisis in which we are presently trapped. Listen to my colleague Henry Stapp's comment on the incredible breakthrough, just over a century ago, in our understanding of the nature of quantum jumps, which are the ultimate events (events, mind you, not things) that constitute reality. This new discovery, Stapp claims,

> induces a profound change in the conception of man's place in the universe. Man can no longer be seen as a deterministically controlled cog in a giant machine. He appears, rather, as an aspect of the fundamental process that gives form and definition to the universe.
>
> The assimilation of this quantum conception of man into the cultural environment of the twenty-first century must

inevitably produce a shift in values conducive to human survival. The quantum conception gives an enlarged sense of self . . . from which must flow lofty values that extend far beyond the confines of narrow personal self-interest.[5]

That man is "a deterministically controlled cog in a giant machine" is the unvarying message of normal science. And "normal" also comes to mean, by an uncritical and unfortunate process, normative. There is undeniably a connection in the prevailing paradigm among all of its major areas of thought and action, a schema we can characterize as:

**Matter Physics → Competition Biology →
Neodarwinian Social Theory**

In other words, the schema that gives us a violent world. Must there not be a similar connection between parallel elements of a new schema:

**Consciousness Physics → Cooperation Biology →
Humane Social Theory**

Which is to say, a nonviolent future, operating on what Marcus Borg has called the "politics of compassion." This revolution is complete as far as theoretical physics is concerned. That is, the "official narrative" of physics (however much actual physicists may ignore it in their daily work) is about a nonlocal, quantum reality rather than the material, reducible "hard" reality of Newton.

And it is the case that, as Willis Harman said, science is the "knowledge validating system" of our culture. Why is it that "normal" behavioral science based on competition and "normal" social theory based on scarcity, violence, and what Kenneth Boulding called "threat power" still rule? Why isn't the paradigm shift happening?

I rarely expose myself voluntarily to mass media, but the other day while I was waiting for a haircut, having neglected to bring something to read, I turned the cover of a large, well-turned-out, and, I might add, relatively progressive magazine. The slick, double-page ad that greeted me was compelling. It showed a strikingly beautiful model lying on her back, her hands thrown casually up behind her head, her back arched—to call her pose suggestive would be an understatement. She looked out at you with half-closed eyes and parted lips, as if she were in the throes of some kind of partnerless ecstasy. Above her stand bold words: "I SENSE, THEREFORE I AM." Descartes must be rolling over in his grave.

And yet, whether Descartes intended it or not, he is now widely held to be the father of the prevailing, rationalist paradigm; and whether the copywriters of the ad intended it as such or not, their slogan is the mantra of our modern civilization, which Toynbee called simply a "sensate civilization." Its implied doctrine—that sense experience delimits the purpose of human existence, indeed of human identity—has created and is perpetuating the spiritual crisis through which we are passing. What I want to do now is put that civilization—its dominating belief that we are separate, material entities in a random universe (and thus condemned to competition and violence), up against that human inheritance called the wisdom tradition. This will put us in a position to come up with some solutions.

Let me begin with a straightforward description of the human being from a well-known text, the Katha Upanishad:

> Senses derive from objects of sense,
> Sense objects from mind,
> Mind from Intellect, and
> Intellect from the principle of individuation [ego, *ahamkāra*],
> Ego from Undifferentiated Consciousness,
> And consciousness from Brahman.
> Brahman is the first cause and final goal.[6]

These words throw into very clear relief what the advertisement I described is doing, as are, of course, hundreds and thousands of other advertisements— according to research by media critic Jean Kilbourne, commercial messages arrive at a rate of 3,000 a day for the average North American.[7] They are creating a culture in which people are encouraged to live at the lowest possible level of reality. It is a powerful culture to which most people in the industrialized world today have effectively no alternative. As anyone who has lived through the collapse of the humanities can tell you, the popular culture that rushed in to fill that vacuum has delivered the vast majority of Americans and their many imitators around the world into the hands of commercial forces that are, in effect, practicing education without a license. In fact, they are doing more: they are creating our culture, although no one in his right mind would have deposited such a sacred trust into such thoughtless hands. This is clearly very dangerous. A sensate civilization (if "civilization" is the word for such a regime) can never satisfy the human being, whose ultimate needs are spiritual; and a frustrated human being will, unless she has a rare capacity for reflection, become a menace to herself and others.

The model of the human person given in the Katha Upanishad has other dimensions. For one thing, the hierarchy of senses, mind, intellect, ego, consciousness, and Brahman is not linear: each higher level yields exponentially greater wisdom, effectiveness, and joy (as other texts spell out). Further, as Plato and medieval scholastics described very well, there are levels of knowing that correspond to these levels of being. Once a person rises above mere sensation, the next higher mode of knowing is knowledge—the acquiring of information. After that comes understanding—the ability to sort facts, see patterns, and make judgments concerning them. Finally, there is wisdom—moral discernment and the will to act in accordance with this discernment (in other words, the cognizance of meaning). So when today we proudly boast that our technology has ushered in the "information age," we are, once again, unwittingly boasting that we are now functioning at the lowest possible level, one step up from animal existence.

But the following consideration is perhaps the most important. What are the creators of the above-mentioned advertisement, with its powerful appeal to an animal drive (for such we would have to call sexuality as they present and use it), doing to us psychologically? Quite simply, they are manipulating our desires. No advertiser, and no professor in Berkeley's splendid new business school, would deny that this is what advertisers do. It's their job description, and business scholars write about how advertising can make people want things they do not want—how, in Gandhi's terms, to make them "multiply their desires." I wonder if any of them realizes how dangerous that is, what an awesome responsibility it entails.

Another juxtaposition may make it clear. I take this famous declaration on the nature of the human being and human desires from another of India's wisest and most ancient texts, the Brihadaranyaka Upanishad:

> A man is what his deep, driving desire is. For as his desire is, so is his will. As his will is, so is his deed. And as his deed is, so is his destiny.[8]

This is an essential insight of the wisdom tradition; it is echoed recently, for instance, by the greatest woman saint of modern India, Anandamayi Ma:

Man appears to be the embodiment of want. Want is what he thinks about and want indeed is what he obtains. Contemplate your true being or else there will be want, wrong action, helplessness, distress and death.[9]

This I consider to be profoundly true; and in so considering it I arrive at the frightening realization that human destiny is being largely controlled today by men and women who are completely unfit for such a responsibility. They do not have, as advertisers, the well-being of their fellows in mind. Not that they are consciously evil—they wouldn't object to our happiness if it didn't interfere with their own—but without being in the least aware of what they're doing, they are ruining our happiness—and their own—by inducing us to misdirect our most precious vital capacity, our desires, into channels which must inevitably lead us to the state Anandamayi Ma describes. Check any newspaper if you do not believe that this is happening. Clearly, one of the things that is blocking human progress today, quite possibly the major thing, is that just when we need a new culture that will help us make a nonlinear leap to a new way of seeing, we have let a powerful new culture-making technology get into the hands of people who have no business using it, people for whom, indeed, such a leap would put them out of a job.

But it is not only advertisers, as we've already seen, who are involved in wreaking havoc on the world without being aware of it. Even "science" as we practice it in this culture is perpetuating a stifling materialism. The problem is not that science has cornered the market on our knowledge of reality—which it arguably deserves—but that it limits itself to what the upanishadic sages call "lower knowledge," where its very success has proven to be its demise:

> Capital finances science, . . . which in turn provides the kind of high technologies that will produce more capital; and so on and so on. Science has become the handmaiden of commerce.[10]

Robert Oppenheimer once said: "The role of science is to make the powers of nature subservient to the human will."[11] On the surface, there may not seem anything wrong with such a project; but a person with some spiritual alertness will immediately ask, "What about that human will we are so interested in empowering?" Recall the chilling description St. Augustine gave us, in four stark words, of the condition of his will prior to his illumination—which is the very condition that the vast majority of us find ourselves in: "Velle meum tenebat inimicus" (The Enemy held my will).

Augustine's explanation has a lot to say about this dangerous condition and about desire, which we have just been emphasizing. "For when libido is pandered to, habit forms; and when habit is not resisted, it becomes compulsion. And it was by these links caught together—which is why I used the image of a chain—that a hard servitude held me fast."[12]

We have placed the elemental forces of nature in the hands of ordinary human beings, dominated as we are by the darker urges, whether we personify them as Augustine does or not. *That* is a spiritual crisis.

Perhaps this does not need further emphasizing, but science can be said to have two functions: to acquire knowledge about the world and to give us power to control it. Neither is dangerous in itself; but clearly, when the second outstrips the first it becomes dangerous indeed. Unfortunately, the knowledge function of science is seriously compromised now because we are *selecting* what we choose to believe science is telling us just as, in quite parallel fashion and with parallel consequences, we select pieces of scripture to justify our own codes of behavior. On any subject that has the slightest bearing on something we need to decide—for example, whether humans are doomed to violence by their nature, or whether there is something called global warming going on—the public will be told reductionist, deterministic, "scientific" findings fully documented by "facts" which they have little ability and perhaps no longer any inclination to verify. The result is that, rather than using the knowledge gained by science to shape policies, to which no one could object, most people use their desires and their will, neither endowment in very good shape right now, to shape "science."

Before moving on to my third question, let me enlist three more juxtapositions that will bring out the connection of all this to violence. In a recent and extremely revealing article in *The New Yorker*, John Saybrook describes his visit to the "lab" in Hollywood where roboticist Stan Winston creates the virtual reality of terror that so many Americans inhabit when they see what are called action movies (and which, not coincidentally, lofted Arnold Schwarzenegger to the role of governor of California). There is much to be learned from this article, for example, how thrilled these technicians are with the emotions of violence—how they find it "inspiring" to, if you'll pardon me, "scare the c__ out of people."[13] And now look at this: "Robots need to display their emotions," a coworker of Winston explained, "so that humans will be able to tell at a glance what's going on inside them." *Emotions? Inside them?* But here's the payoff. Soon, in the U.S. and Japan, there will be too many old people to take care of, say the monster-makers. "The solution could be a sociable robot, something that lives with you and that you can have *a meaningful emotional relationship* with."[14] Utter blindness to what René Girard calls the "true nature of violence," namely that it is wrong and hurtful, and that violence and dehumanization go hand in hand. Invite the latter, for whatever misconceived reason, and you will never be able to escape the former.

My second juxtaposition concerns the official policy of the United States as now articulated in our National Security Document in three ringing words: Full Spectrum Dominance. Now, Saint Augustine too offers a ringing formula, this one in only two words which he repeats throughout the beginning sections of the *City of God* because they delineate the root cause of human evil, the basis of all our wars and strife—*vis dominandi*—the lust to dominate. Not to put too fine a point on it, our nation has explicitly, in full ignorance of what it is doing, adopted the root cause of evil as our national purpose. I cannot find words adequate to comment on this dangerous folly.

Finally, let me quote the justification, or if you prefer the cocky attempt at reassurance, offered by the President in the face of the isolation of the country from most of the international community during the run-up to the present Iraq war: "At some point, we may be the only ones left. That's okay with me. We are America."[15]

I have to point out, as a trained reader of texts, the highly expressive, probably not conscious use of pronouns in this amazing utterance. Since "That's okay with me" (not, for example, with the American people) comes right before "We are America," one cannot escape the implication of *l'état c'est moi*, a view which would in fact be consistent with a good deal of this President's speech and behavior. In other words, just under the surface of his words, the President is hinting that the "we" in the last ringing phrase is royal. He thinks he is the country. We are not amused.

But to bring out the full implications of this narcissism I would like to juxtapose this remark with a passage from the sixteenth book of the *Iliad*. Homer is not usually considered a wisdom writer, and I'm not arguing for an upgrade, but there is certainly a kind of wisdom in these lines, which the poet has placed in the mouth of Achilles, who is sending his companion Patroclus into battle:

Oh father Zeus, Athena and Apollo, let not one
    Trojan escape death, many though they be,
Nor a single Argive, but may we two emerge safe
    from destruction, Thus to strip down alone the
    bright ramparts of Troy.[16]

The characters in Greek epic are typological, like those of the Mahabharata (where we are on safer ground thanks to a sophisticated native tradition of interpretation). That is, while being fully fleshed out as distinct individuals (for which Homer had a rare genius), they also represent what we might call karmic types. And thanks to Simone Weil, we know that Achilles represents the dual devotion to death—to killing and being killed—that is the defining feature of the warrior ethos.[17] Some years ago I took this classic analysis of Weil's a step further when I uncovered what is probably the reason for the puzzling rivalry between Achilles and his fellow Argive warrior, Odysseus. Odysseus will return home and reenter family and society—he stands for that destiny; Achilles, by contrast, is dedicated to sacrificial death for the community (which community he ironically hates, perhaps for that reason). He can never survive

OUR SPIRITUAL CRISIS

21

battle because his entire typological purpose is to die there.[18] (I might add that when the press regularly refers to any American wounded or killed in Iraq as a "hero," they are unconsciously but quite deliberately appealing to the same sacralization.)

The lines just quoted occur, as I say, in the famous speech the hero makes to his companion, Patroclus, when his game plan of staying out of the battle to enhance his private status starts to go oddly wrong. He sends Patroclus (who on the typological level is a kind of ritual substitute for the hero) into the field in his stead. It is in fact in this very speech that Achilles seals his fate by clinching his identity as the warrior-sacrifice who will never return home to build the social order; and the lines that I've just quoted are its climax. His shocking prayer that his enemies, the Trojans, be not just defeated but annihilated, *and* that the same fate befall his "companions," the Argives, to clear the path to his own glory, brings out the stark isolation and the destructiveness of his path.

If one starts from the underlying logic of competition (of which the logic of war is the extreme conclusion), I do not think one can long avoid ending up at this startling wish of Achilles—that all his fellow fighters perish. The wildly successful television show *Survivor* also perfectly embodies this wish: to be *numero uno*. But, as we have seen, to be numero uno finally means to be *solo*, utterly, existentially alone. Achilles stands for the ultimate value system of violence, here stripped of its usual disguises of service to the community and glory. We see here how the reliance on violence and the values of violence are inherently narcissistic; conversely, narcissism is a form of violence to the human spirit, for it is our inescapable nature—although we seem to be trying to escape it in every possible way, "to seek fellowship and as far as we possibly can, peace with every man," as Augustine said in the first articulate description of peace in Western literature—and there is therefore no fault more harmful, echoes a modern mystic, than "the fault of separateness."[19]

Think back, for a moment, to the young lady in the slick magazine. It is interesting that it would be difficult to translate her mantra back into Latin. You would want to say "sentio ergo sum," but "sentio" is a transitive verb. It means to perceive *something*; whereas our model is not saying that she is perceiving anything, just that she is *having a sensation*. Her narcissism is complete. Christopher Lasch warned us back in 1979 that we were creating a "culture of narcissism."[20] What I have been trying to show are the inevitable political results of that long-outworn but still oppressively dominant culture.

We were encouraged after 9/11 to connect the dots in order better to protect ourselves in the future. I submit that the kind of thinking we have just been doing connects a very different set of dots, and will do that job much better: we are looking not laterally, to trace precisely which people delivered which attack, but down into the layers of causality from the political world to the culture that sustains that style of politics, and finally deeper, to the spiritual emptiness that has allowed such a culture to reach such proportions today. At bottom, we have forgotten that we are human beings—that we are consciousness and life inhabiting a physical body, spirit disguised as body. And what makes us forget it is a culture that has propelled most of us into a hopeless search for self-gratification through sensation. As long as such a culture prevails, how can we expect not to promote and to experience violence, for example, by elevating to high office those who know no alternative?

QUESTION THREE

What, then, can we do to bring about the paradigm shift to a world based on consciousness, cooperation, and peace? For there is no doubt that such a shift is incipient: the fact that we are discussing it here is evidence, however small, of such a shift trying to happen. As we know from the work of Paul Ray and Sherry Anderson, what we have been discussing here tonight represents the aspiration of millions of people in this country alone.[21] We know that the present direction of society is creating widespread misery, generating an enormous pressure to seek *some* kind of change—and we know that extreme directional shifts can happen. What's not entirely clear is how. Short of divine intervention—which we cannot rule out, but which we cannot expect to occur without some signal from our side—what can individuals do to precipitate the shift?

Of course, the shift we need is huge; it demands a spiritual growth spurt. And so it is reasonable to ask, can religion play a role in facilitating it? Intuitively we want to say, "How could it not?" But as we know to our cost, "religious" does not necessarily mean "spiritual." What would religions themselves need to do in order to respond to this need? Here I would like to submit a model I have found useful as a way to understand the evolution of human consciousness in terms of religion. In these terms I think our evolution can be said to pass through three general stages. To distinguish between these stages, we can, for the sake of simplicity, take as our criterion the place where worshippers locate power. Where do they feel ultimate reality resides, and, therefore, what power does their religion seek to propitiate and use?

In the first stage, that power was felt to reside in living nature (a power we fall short of describing when we blandly call it "the environment"). In the second stage, power is felt to reside in the community, although the gods of nature are not left completely behind, since this is a cumulative type of evolution, when it works well. And in the third, decisive stage, power is finally felt to reside in the individual. The long road has led from an awareness of reality outside, through a sort of "intersubjective" stage in which the tribe or city-state or other community is the focus of reverence and legitimacy, to the "modern" discovery of reality within.

The first stage is prehistoric, but you can see clear traces of it in many surviving communities and animistic religions. Some of those which continue today in Japan are successful descendants of this. The second is instantly recognizable as the religion of the ancient Western world, Greece and Rome, where every political entity from the family to the city-state (and the larger, but loosely affiliated *ethnos*) had its god. This is commonly called "paganism." And the third stage? As far as the West is concerned, it was, or was supposed to be, the religion of Jesus. The execution of Jesus by the Roman state was a horrific act of violence that I believe had a divine purpose in human history: it sent a powerful message that the state itself as the focus of human worship, the seat of the sacred, was "a creed outworn," a dangerous superstition. For this reason, the terrific struggles of the early Church, and of all those who subsequently rediscovered Jesus's nonviolent message down to our present day, have always involved a tension between the individual conscience and the state. Indeed, this was probably the content of Jesus's own struggle against the centralized temple worship of the Jewish world.[22]

We think monotheism can be defined as that stage in the evolution of consciousness when the human being comes to conceive of God—the supreme reality—as One. That is correct; but monotheism is simultaneously the discovery of the sanctity of the individual. It may be hard to remember this in our overpopulated world where there are more than six billion such individuals. Yet when monotheism was discovered in the appropriation by the West of the

Jewish religion as consummated by Jesus (a paradigm shift if there ever was one), the integrity of the human individual—that is, our unity and consequently our inherent sanctity—became an inescapable corollary. In Kant's words, it is the supreme reality without and the same reality within. We cannot even say which discovery came first, the discovery that the individual is sacred or that God is One. But in either case it is clear that the state and its institutions of domination, such as the death penalty and war, have got to be overcome for this precious new insight to be realized.

How does this help us see the present crisis in context? To put it very simply, we are stage-three people living in a stubbornly stage-two world. Sometimes we complain, as I did here this evening, that the popular conception of physics is a hundred years out of date. Well, to worship the state as God and to deny the primacy of the individual, not to mention the rights of the individual, has been out of date for 2,000 years!

A slight digression is in order. There is a story (I think I read it in Hans-Joachim Schoeps) that when Napoleon was on his imperial roll, bidding fair to conquer the world, a scholar came to him with a plan for a new religion. Napoleon is said to have thanked him, and replied, "Now go out and get crucified." Changes of this kind do not come for being planned by a few intellectuals, or adventurers, and you may be wondering, indeed I myself am wondering, what authority I (who do not even belong to a denominational religion) have to make these suggestions. Yet, despite Napoleon's wise advice, I feel called to make this sweeping generalization about modern religion, and to take it a step further. It is the step from belief to practice. What shift in the practice of worship is implied by the shift I claim to see from the former to the desired new kind of religion? It seems to me to follow that, we need to change from a religion based on sacrifice, which suited perfectly a stage-two religion's dedication the state's identity and power, to a religion based on meditation, which is needed in a system that seeks instead to develop and release into society the power of the individual. Today it is not so much the unity-of-God aspect of a stage-three religion that is of operational significance as is the integrity, the fundamental reality (i.e., sanctity) of the person. Since most people do not really believe in God, despite claims to the contrary, it does not much matter whether they disbelieve in one God or many. But it matters a great deal who we think *we* are and how we should relate to each other.

You will be surprised, perhaps, that I think we still *have* a sacrificial religion. I wish I had more time to develop this, but I was hinting about it in my suggestion of a line of descent that goes from Achilles to George Bush. There is a part of René Girard's work that I feel to be profoundly and inescapably true, and that is the connection he draws between the ritual of lethal sacrifice that was the source of power in pagan religion (or in my terms, stage-two religion) to medieval pogroms and to many modern forms of the same deadly dynamic that are now disguised as secular acts, such as the death penalty, lynching, and many others. Why else would the death penalty oddly persist in the world's most violent democracy, even though it has been proven not to work?

The stage-three equivalent of the sacrifice is meditation. Let me fall back on Augustine to hint, at least, at what I mean:

> In their impious pride . . . these scholars [who predict eclipses and so forth] do not give themselves to you so that you may preserve what you have made, nor do they slay in your honor those selves of their own making, nor immolate their high-flown pride as though it were a sacrifice of birds, nor make into an offering of fish that curiosity whereby they walk the secret pathways of the deep, nor sacrifice their self-indulgent habits like beasts of the field, so that you, O God . . . may consume their dead ambitions and re-create the seekers for eternal life.[23]

Augustine does not reject the sacrifice, but internalizes it. We are to make an offering not of some external beast but of the "bestiality" that may still lurk within us. What are to be controlled are our own negative drives and qualities, our *vasanas* as the Buddha called them, which make up our separate selves. Like all that we are, they are the result of our thoughts—our mental impulses, our feelings—and the only way these can be controlled, at least in the modern world, if not any world, is through the supreme *yajña*, or sacrifice, that meditation was long ago recognized to be in India. I was pleased to learn recently that some seventy-five colleges and universities in the United States now have programs of some kind in contemplative practices.[24] Colleges and universities are not the ideal places to learn such practices, but given what else goes on in the American university today, one can hardly complain if some of its efforts are going toward developing a mode of knowing that is above rather than below the intellect.

In making this plea I hope not to be entirely guilty of the hubris Napoleon warned of, for I am really directing it at individuals within religions rather than religions themselves (though I would applaud the introduction of meditation in Western, institutional religions—and I have just returned from a meeting with some Benedictine nuns in Europe for that purpose). We need not hesitate to focus on the individual as the locus of change: what could be more appropriate to a stage-three environment?

When movements fail, when governments backslide, when every kind of organization, even universities, is being reinvented as a corporation and corporations have shown their deafness to human needs, what do we do? We look for the power to change where we should have looked for it in the first place, in the individual—in us. The now officially blessed Mother Teresa had it right: "ek, ek, ek" (one by one); it's the only way we can go and the only way we need go. She did not mean, nor do I mean, the isolated individual into which American individualism can degenerate (though we hardly have a monopoly); she meant the sacred individual whose depth connects with the reality of all others. If totalitarianism, as Hannah Arendt taught, "strives not toward despotic rule over men but toward a system in which men are superfluous," then our task is to make men and women the very center of our thinking, our concerns, and our values.

My emphasis on meditation will raise a question that is pertinent to all of us, particularly those who, like myself, believe that the situation we are in will require some kind of more-than-human intervention. Recognizing the need for more-than-human intervention does not, however, mean that there is no human element involved. On the contrary, as mentioned briefly above, a comfortable consensus of humanity's greatest teachers holds that if we do everything we can, we may make ourselves eligible, so to speak, for a matching grant of more-than-matching, utterly decisive potency. What kind of voice should we be raising in this wilderness? Or how should we be raising it? I put the question because in our pluralistic religious consciousness today there are often two complementary techniques of inner communion: meditation and prayer. What is the relationship between them, between the meditation, which we not very accurately associate with the practice of Eastern religions, and the practice of prayer we associate with ours? As it happens, there is one man of prayer in the modern world who bridges these cultures perfectly, namely Mahatma Gandhi, and he is just the one we would hope to consult about a shift away from violence. Prayer was "the staff of his life," as he often maintained, but he was equally adamant that in order for prayer to be effective, it would have to meet three criteria:

1. It has to be selfless (petitionary prayer is okay if it is selfless).
2. We have to make the prayer with complete concentration.
3. We must have some awareness that the Power we are addressing is within us.

Seen in this light, prayer and meditation (or complete concentration) converge. Gandhi, in fact, said as much on at least one occasion: "True meditation consists in closing the eyes and ears of the mind to all else except the object of one's devotion. Hence the closing eyes during prayer is an aid to such concentration."[25]

If there is one thing that the pluralistic religious environment of our country (in particular) should teach us today, it is that a plea for interior practice directed toward a more-than-human Reality, call it meditation or concentrated prayer, though I have made bold to claim that no truly modern religion can be without it, does not replace outer work. Contemplation and action are not an either/or proposition, and here recall the old story about a preceptor who was asked by his students which they should do, since if everything depends on God there should be no need to work and if everything depends on them there is no need to pray. He answered them, "Pray as if everything depended on God and work as if everything depended on you." And since we must do both, I would like to complement what we've just been saying with a final suggestion: that everyone today needs to have a working knowledge of nonviolence. As Martin Luther King Jr. said, Gandhi is "essential," and "we ignore him at our peril." Here is why: If we do not have a working knowledge of the dynamics of principled nonviolence, of at least the most useful models that have been developed to explain that science so far, we will have no alternative to put alongside the conquest model of security to which people in the cultural mainstream are now clinging so desperately. Without anything else to hold on to, they will cling to that model until it kills them (and likely the rest of us, who will not be eligible for the Rapture). But in addition, without a sense of precisely how nonviolence works, those who throw themselves, sometimes passionately, into the search for peace often do so, in my observation, passionately but inaccurately. This would not be the place to go into details, so I may be allowed to refer the reader to my recent book and web site for specificity on this crucial point.[26]

This we know about the mysterious ways of the paradigm: no alternative, no shift. No matter how outmoded the old paradigm has become, no matter how dangerous, there must be an alternative before one can abandon it. No one is Kierkegaardian enough to step off into the void and stand paradigmless before the white light of unconditioned Reality. I was therefore very pleased that my colleagues at Youngstown State University, where I spoke recently, pulled the following line from my recent book as the motto for their upcoming conference: "The point is not to stop war, but to start nonviolence."

Without nonviolence, nothing that we solve will stay solved. With nonviolence, a lot of it will solve itself.

Those of us who feel disinclined to get crucified (and I count myself in that vast majority) can, nonetheless, make a significant contribution to the regeneration of our world by becoming "nonviolence-literate." Of course, some people who would not be able to articulate the first thing about nonviolence nonetheless use it to great effect, and God bless them. Still, it does seem to me that right now for the Big Shift to happen we need an articulate, scientific model of this great force. It is at least *a*, and possibly *the* missing item to facilitate the impending paradigm shift. Gandhi was as far ahead of our time as Jesus was of his; but we don't have another 2,000 years to catch up with him.

Commentary by
Lewis S. Mudge

THANK YOU, MICHAEL, for that brilliant and truly engaging paper. I think that what we are trying to do here is create a space of "resonance" between our diverse faiths with reference to their public implications. We hope to respond to each other in terms of the ways our souls are "tuned." This despite the rather large differences among the tunes we hear. I, for example, am a Christian theologian and ethicist. Interreligiously I work mainly among the "religions of the book," Judaism, Christianity, and Islam. If I can judge from the number of saffron robes I see out there, faiths other than those three are well represented among us tonight. What I have to say will inevitably use a vocabulary different and difficult for some, if only too familiar to others.

I like to think of conversations like this one as enacting a kind of mutual moral and spiritual "hospitality." Professor David Ford, a Christian theologian at Cambridge University in England, put it this way just a few years back. He asked,

> how might [theologians and scholars in religious studies] appropriately celebrate the millennium? A simple yet rich answer is by being guests and hosts. A theology under the sign of hospitality is formed through its generous welcome to others—theologies, traditions, disciplines, and spheres of life. It has the host's responsibility for homemaking, the hard work of preparation, and the vulnerability of courteously offering something while having little control over its reception. It also has the different responsibility of being a guest, trying to be sensitive to strange households, learning complex codes and

risking new food and drink. Ideally, habitual hospitality gives rise to trust and friendship in which new exchanges can plumb the depths of similarity, difference, and suffering.[27]

We come, whether as hosts or as guests, from different religious traditions. But we are wrestling in the name of those traditions with the common problems of humanity in our time. While remaining faithful in thought and practice to our spiritual communities, many of us, like yourself, Michael, have also taken responsibility—beyond job description, beyond routine—for doing what we can about the many threats to life that beset our planet. And we have taken the risk of meeting others different from ourselves who have done the same. We are, despite our differences, "rooted responsibility-takers," or, as someone has said, "rooted cosmopolitans." We seek continuing sustenance from the spiritual soils in which we are rooted while seeking to be citizens of this very diverse and contentious world.

It is my guess that, in doing this, or in even conceiving what it might mean to do this, we are members of rather small minorities in our faith communities. We are (dare I say it?) various sorts of liberal intellectuals. Not everyone interprets his or her faith traditions the way we do. I can speak only for myself as a Christian. I believe that far too many Christians allow themselves to be used by political leaders who speak the language of faith but have self-serving purposes in mind. You may read my mind for examples if you like! Such influence usually pushes faith traditions in a rightward direction. I think that the same happens, in varying degrees, in faiths other than my own. Among other things, politicians incite us to violence against one another. Elements in faith traditions that countenance violence are exploited for political reasons, while the more peaceful elements are downplayed. This is a matter of hermeneutics, or theory of interpretation, of which more in a minute.

Professor Samuel Huntington of Harvard argued a few years back that the next half-century will be one of religiously inspired warfare on a global scale. He began with the observation that each one of the nine great "civilizations" of humankind has religious origins. But, instead of sharing spiritual insight, they compete violently. They press up against one another like tectonic places. The crunch points produce earthquakes, volcanoes, and tidal waves. You can see the results along the fault lines of the Balkans, the Middle East, Northern Ireland, Indonesia, and myriad other places.

Rooted responsibility-takers are religious people who, in the name of the whole of humanity, resist letting themselves or their traditions be used in this way. Instead, they engage with various totalizing ideologies—political and economic ones especially—on behalf of the human race. But, while reactionary forces are well organized, well financed, and know what they want, the forces of resistance to injustice and exploitation are fragmented, underfinanced, and have little agreement about what they want. There are not enough of us around. But, even worse, we do not know one another *as* the rooted responsibility-takers we hope to be. We do not even share with one another the meaning of worldly responsibility-taking in the light of religious tradition.

A world-historical task of our time is to get these resistance forces, some of which we represent here tonight, effectively together around common practices and goals. We could *covenant* with one another *not* to be taken in by political adventurers. We could become, together, a kind of "third force" in the world given neither to blind, isolated, angry traditionalism nor to the purely secular pursuit of profit and political advantage. We could share an effort to mobilize the "soul force" (as Gandhi put it) of our various spiritualities for the common good.

I do not mean to advocate a simple kind of syncretism. I said "mobilize." I didn't say "assimilate." What I am talking about is not a combination that might purport to be some sort of new religion, but rather mutual recognition that each of us, with our different roots and commitments, is having an experience parallel or analogous with that of others in seeking to grapple with the follies and injustices of our day. I mean that if we are Hindus or Buddhists— or otherwise—who are trying to be rooted public-responsibility-takers—then we need to recognize that there are at least a few Jews, Christians, and Muslims trying to be and do the same thing. I mean a kind of recognition of parallel struggles across the different faith traditions and a kind of recognition that together we could be a force the world desperately needs.

I have been working on this idea in a context which may seem rather restricted to this multifaith audience. I've been trying to encourage what I call the practice of "parallel hermeneutics" among the "religions of the book," Judaism, Christianity, and Islam. I do not forget "Eastern religions," but sometimes one must not try to do too much at once. The religions of the book have in common the patriarch Abraham, even as they interpret him in quite varying, even competitive ways. But all agree that Abraham was an honest, faithful man who did not worship idols. He represents a kind of primordial religious and moral ideal that all three faiths can and do recognize as standing at their origins.

Above all, Abraham is faithful to a covenantal promise which proves to be a promise to all humankind. The closing line of it in Genesis 12:1–3 says that in Abraham and Sarah's posterity "all the families of the earth will find blessing." The biblical writer could not have imagined how many families of the earth there would eventually be. But here is the charter of common blessing to humanity that our interpretations of tradition should now be aiming at.

I speak of *parallel* hermeneutics: independent practices of interpretation carried on side by side, launching different religious traditions on paths leading in the same direction. Not one single interpretative practice, not one single path, but comparable practices near enough together that we can call out to one another and feel companionship along the way. I cannot become you, nor can you become me. But it means something to me that I believe your experience is analogous with mine, parallel with mine, and mine with yours. There can be no "blessing" unless we work together. Carried on separately, our work contradicts the goal we seek.

Perhaps the very idea of "blessing," as opposed to "curse," can help this perspective reach beyond the too-often violent "religions of the book" to invite a degree of resonance among the more peaceful religions of the East. Although I cannot vouch for the accuracy of his Hebrew exegesis, I like these words of Matthew Fox:

> As Rabbi Heschel puts it, "Just to be is a blessing; just to live is holy." It is telling that the Hebrew word for blessing, *berakah,* is closely related to the word for create, *bara.* . . . This suggests that a creation is necessarily a blessing, is wrapped up as a blessing. . . . Furthermore, the very word for blessing in Hebrew also means "pool," and with the change of one vowel, to *berekah,* the word means a reservoir where camels kneel for a resting place. The images of pool and reservoir created by desert people tell us all we need to know about the desirability behind a theology of blessing. The word for covenant is also directly related to the words for "create" and for "blessing." A covenant is a blessing agreement, a promise to bless and to return blessing for blessing.[28]

I suppose that I am very Western in seeing the covenantal gift that Abraham and Sarah receive as one of responsibility to this promise of universal blessing. But I believe that such responsibility is not confined to readers of the Hebrew Bible. For it rests first upon the gift of conscious agency that we receive in being created as persons. What are awareness, and the ability to act, *for* in the cosmic evolutionary scheme? They are for the purpose of giving us human beings some responsibility for what happens next. The account in Genesis is one version *of* something we all share, even if we express it in widely different ways.

And finally, Michael, since I feel such a wide area of agreement with what you have shared with us, may I ask you to comment on how someone in my position might make direct use of it. For I sense that your three proposals for doing this are going to be rather ineffectual as far as Western societies are concerned. Individuality and nonviolence and the articulating work of intellectuals sit well with us in this room. But I want to see a new spiritual paradigm happen in society generally. And the one way in which I think I have any way of making an impact is through those millions of people who sit Sunday mornings in pews. How do I or we get under their skins?

Response and
Audience
Discussion

Michael Nagler: Well, Lew, that is a challenging question, and I think I have a challenging answer to offer you before I back up and respond to some of the many excellent points you raise. Here's my challenge, which I'll couch in Gandhi's language. Why could not parishioners, certainly in the more progressive and open-minded communities to which you have access, spend some time making what Gandhi called "a reverent study of all religions"? That would in no way diminish their faith in or commitment to their own religion. As Gandhi testified, his Hinduism was the stronger for his reverent study of Islam, Christianity, and so forth. As Emperor Ashoka said, "He who has no respect for another's religion has no respect for his own." Who can be considered remotely educated today if he or she does not have enough knowledge of other religions to understand how his or her own fits into the scheme of things? More particularly, what will happen to us if we are so ignorant of Islam that we cannot evaluate the inflammatory nonsense we are being subjected to about that faith and its adherents?

And for a second suggestion, they can learn the history and the theory of nonviolence. They're not going to get it in school! They're not going to get it, needless to say, from television! What better place to get it in than the houses of God? We at the Blue Mountain Center have been working on this idea, and I'm happy to report that our book on Gandhi, *Gandhi the Man*, is being used as the core of a seven-week church program by Unity churches around the country and is posted on their website (www.unityofthevalley.org).

In this connection, Lew, I want to personally thank you for the inspiring, and insightful sketch you have drawn of the possibilities for cooperation today among religious communities, a cooperation that could and should lead to much greater peace on this planet of ours—quite the reverse, indeed, of Professor Huntington's dire prognostications!

On listening to you I was reminded, not without a thrill of recognition, of the observation made by Gilbert Murray in his magisterial history of Greek literature that toward the end of pagan antiquity, an educated pagan was so much the monotheist (or perhaps crypto-monotheist if conditions demanded) that he had more in common with a Christian than with his frankly polytheistic coreligionists, who were such in name only. It strikes me that today, as we stand before a change that will be no less cataclysmic than the shift of the ancient world from a state-based to a person-based world order (I am of course putting my own emphasis on this change), a change of similar content and magnitude but hopefully of less violent process, that again we people of the book have more in common with our yellow-robed brothers and sisters who believe, like us, in the sanctity of the human spirit, than we have with our nominal coreligionists who fear the "other" and would use the arts of violence to keep them at bay. I am thrilled by the prospect of making this bond between us real, by acting it out among ourselves and on the world around us, and by our newly exercised strength bring along with us those for whom fear and confusion have come to dominate their minds and block up the springs of love within them.

You called us "rooted responsibility-takers," and I love that phrase. It recalls to my mind the way the citizens of Le Chambon who, under the direction of their brave pastor André Trocmé and his wife Magda banded together to rescue thousands of Jewish and other refugees during the stark years of the occupation, modestly referred to themselves: *les responsables*. Conversely, it is so clear that the gathering evils around us today depend absolutely on the abdication of moral judgment by people who have, in all fairness to them, been relentlessly trained to abdicate moral judgment, if not all human judgment, by our culture of greed and sensation. I have absolute faith that if we who hold the faith that we hold in humanity above all differences of sect or tradition, including those of us who claim adherence to no formal sect or tradition, can reassure and utterly win over those who have been frightened out of their sense of responsibility, if not out of their senses entirely, we can build a better world with them. What is required of us is to manifest that higher vision, the vision that unites us at our human core. I would imagine that we have to manifest it by working it out in thought, as we are all doing here tonight, and by grounding it in our hearts by spiritual practice, and by witnessing to it when to do so requires risk and sacrifice—almost a kind of martyrdom, if you will, if not at the level required by Napoleon!—and by institutionalizing it in our societies and the common society toward which humanity is groping.

One of the precious insights I learned early on from my teacher, and it was almost embarrassingly simple for the self-appointed intellectual that I conceived myself to be at that time, was that all religions converge in practice while they diverge, and at times quite appropriately, in dogma. That is, both in the practices they teach that lead to God-consciousness for those who are ready to undertake that ascent and the practices of loving-kindness among our fellows that would bring a "City of God" on our Earth. (He did not mean ritual practices, but those also have a commonality at the core underneath their infinite variety). We of the book may say, "Thou shalt not murder," while the Hindu-Buddhist tradition may come at it more positively and say, "Nonviolence is the highest law,"[29] but is anyone going to say that these civilizations began from an essentially different insight into human nature, or derived a contrasting norm therefrom? So it is precisely from these great truths that we share in common, and which all people have as their deepest yearnings though some are not aware of it, that we ought to proceed to build this new community and new order. (There are, of course, groups like the United Religions Initiative already at work at this). In other words, the more we put the core vision of our religion, whatever it is, into practice in our daily lives, the more the differences among our faiths will fade into insignificance (and Professor Huntington's prediction along with them).

Having said that, though, I very much appreciate what you imparted about the etymology of the Hebrew word "bless," making it very real as a conferring of life-energy on something or someone. This certainly compares favorably with our own word "bless," from the Gothic, meaning "to sprinkle with blood"![30] Pure stage two, leading us directly back into the world of unanimous violence.

All of which brings me to your last, practical point, without which our speculations might end up being amusing at best and at worst distractions at a time when we can least afford them. Where do we go with all this?

First of all, I quite agree with you that when people come together, even if it be once a week to absent themselves from the cares of the world for a time, to hear words of inspiration in community, it is an ideal context in which to air the insights we've been discussing. I've mentioned how one denomination is already doing this. What is the task?

Well, there is an intellectual, cognitive job that has to be done, but this is the relatively easy part to talk about. I believe in my heart that the spiritual discipline piece is the core without which no change will be lasting, but I won't say more about it because it is in the nature of the case an individual matter. (Not to mention that I happen to be nowhere near a spiritual teacher). But study also is necessary, and churchgoers can do it in two ways. They can undertake what Gandhi called "a reverent study" of all religions, and similarly of nonviolence.

But let me put this suggestion in a wider context, because after the first appearance of *Search for a Nonviolent Future* (or its original title, *Is There No Other Way?*) I was repeatedly asked what people could do about the extreme danger in which we find ourselves, and I came up with a list of five things that can be done by anyone (focusing unapologetically on the individual rather than on organizations):

1. Insulate ourselves as far as humanly possible from the effects of the commercial mass media. Simply put: boycott them. They serve no purpose other than deception. Far better news is now available via the internet (including emails from those we trust) and infinitely better, nonvirtual entertainment is available from *people*. Take a friend to lunch. It's better than a movie, anytime.

   Perhaps this is worth repeating because it's as important, as it is—to some of us at least— surprising: Epictetus said, "The only thing you can control, and therefore the only thing you need to control, is the imagery in your own mind." Right now the imagery in our own minds is being controlled by those who own the commercially driven mass media, the motives of which I need not subject to further scrutiny.

2. Take up some form of spiritual discipline appropriate to oneself. This is an individual matter and I've said enough about it perhaps already, but I warmly invite anyone interested to have a look at the website of the Blue Mountain Center of Meditation, my own spiritual community, which is www.nilgiri.org.

3. Act out the changes that steps 1 and 2 will bring about in our life—no matter on what scale. Dehumanization, remember, is the essence of violence. We are living in an increasingly dehumanizing world, from the solipsism of commercial culture (which paradoxically diminishes the meaning of the individual it seeks to exalt) to the careless claims of scientists who seem to enjoy thinking of us, and by extension themselves, as machines. Rehumanization, then, is a powerful antidote; and fortunately rehumanization can be done by something as simple as civility and genuine sympathy in daily interactions. As Mother Teresa put it, "Say yes to peace with your tongue. Close your mouth rather than speaking a word which will hurt anyone."[31] I support that and have elaborated on it in *Search for a Nonviolent Future*.

4. The big surprise: "learn nonviolence." You may feel that I have said enough about this already,

RESPONSE AND DISCUSSION

but I do feel that in today's environment it needs reemphasis. (As Max Müller used to say, "there are some truths worth repeating until everyone believes them.") And finally,

5. Get involved in peace work. There are several guidelines that will help one focus this work effectively listed in my longer version of these suggestions on www.mettacenter.org, along with my favorite candidate for a peace project to join, the Nonviolent Peaceforce (www.nonviolentpeaceforce.org).

I hope you see some merit in these suggestions for individuals, whether parishioners or not. In any case, thank you again for the question.

DISCUSSION WITH AUDIENCE

Question (from Huston Smith): How do you square the notion of evolutionary consciousness with the Hindu doctrine of the Four Yugas, which is one of decline?

Nagler: I do not think there is a very good way to square those two things, regrettably, because I have often puzzled over that contradiction. Now it happens to be the case, and this is only something we have realized recently, that the Four Yugas doctrine, stating that the world process is a continuous deterioration down to this present age of violence, is relatively recent. It seems to appear first in well-developed form in the Mahabharata, which puts in about the 2nd century BCE. It is not a Vedic doctrine.

However that may be, perhaps the way the two evolutionary models are to be reconciled, really, is not to take the timeframes too literally, but rather to see them as the "story" of two forces which are acting on us in the present. One, the downward force, which is the after-echo of the Big Bang, so to speak, is driving us apart and further from our spiritual reality—what brought the world into existence according to the Hindu cosmology was the primordial desire for separateness. We are still experiencing, clearly, the momentum of that desire. But that very desire brings about its opposite: the inevitable yearning to recover and return to wholeness. And we live in tension between those two. So that means to me that perhaps the time frames here are symbolic rather than real. Thus, we should think about living in the crux of those two conflicting desires, and having the responsibility given to us as human beings of making the choice which desire to align ourselves with.

Huston Smith: You did me the honor of referring to the wisdom tradition, but am I wrong in thinking that they all have consciousness as basic, and the reversal of this belief came only in the seventeenth century? Now if they had what you would like to see us appropriate, and I would too, why then, how much difference is that going to make, because in their behavior did they *behave* any better? There's a Chinese saying that I have written in calligraphy hanging over my door, and I regard it often as it so nurtures my spirit every time I regard it. It says: "tian di you qing" (Heaven and earth possess sentience). The reason I treasure this saying so much is not simply for the beautiful lettering, but because of its meaning: that the whole world is pervaded with spirit. This is most wonderful. So, I am all for the paradigm shift, though I think it is a kind of going back to what we had before this aberration, but I am not confident that is going to do us good. It will do us good in the long run, if we *have* a long run.

Nagler: This is a very fair and very tough question, Huston. So you said that the wisdom tradition has always maintained that consciousness is primary. I have never had any problem with the wisdom tradition itself; I think what I was talking about is the degree to which it has been assimilated at various stages. In a stage-two religion there was a kind of built-in limit as to how well it could be assimilated, because of the exteriorization of the religious concept and belief that the central reality was the political entity of the community, whose "consciousness" is only a metaphor, really a projection of the consciousness of the human beings who create what Richard Barnet called this "mystique" of a state. This was the clash between Socrates, who realized that however much he loved his city (the state of that time) it could not override individual conscience, and the state, which thought that it should do just that. So you are exactly right, I am not talking about a new wisdom tradition by any stretch of the imagination; I am talking about a new model to assimilate what has always been there in the wisdom tradition. I am trying to get at what are the elements we need now to open us up to that tradition. There may be a slightly new *form*—I guess the form of the tradition is always new—but the essential insight that consciousness is primary is, as we say, perennial. And to respond to your second, and most urgent point, I do believe that the rediscovery of this perennial truth right now, by and for us, would bring with it a redemption from violence. Would this be "the millennium" in the sense that we would fix the human problem for all time? I very much doubt it. But it could be like those other historical moments that experienced the freshness of rediscovery, when violence in fact was for a time considerably reduced. It would give us a desperately needed chance at recovery and setting the human experiment back on track.

Thank you, by the way, Huston, for helping me with this clarification.

Question: There seems to be widely varying ideas about what "nonviolence" is. Some people think nonviolence is just about humans; whereas some people, especially today, consider it to apply to all beings. What is your position on this?

Nagler: There are really two issues here: (1) what do we think nonviolence is; and (2) how far should we extend it? When I use the term "principled nonviolence" I am arguing for the conception of nonviolence as a positive force which is generated in human consciousness. It is akin to what I was saying previously about monotheism being officially the discovery that God is One somewhere up there in the sky, but in reality is an allegory for the discovery of the integral and sacred nature of the individual. Nonviolence is a little like that; that is to say, we realize that nonviolence has got be driven deeply down into every impulse of our being, and that is simultaneously to realize that we cannot stop the application of it anywhere. In fact, this was part of René Gerard's discovery (and of our own Ursula LeGuin, and many others) that as long as paradise is predicated on the elimination of somebody, or some group, it is flawed (and hence not paradise). As St. Augustine said, "If you dislike anyone or anything, you are denying God." So Gandhi's model was that the individual serves the family, the family serves the village, the village serves the district, the district serves the nation, and the nation serves the world. And this created what he called the "oceanic circle," and it extended everywhere. And—to answer your question, finally!—yes, it would reach out to all sentient beings. And in the end, as Einstein says, to "the whole of nature in its beauty"—which, if you pursue the logic we are developing here, is in some way also sentient. Hence Huston Smith's calligraphy!

Question: There are many Buddhists here tonight who might be wondering about the dualism of your presentation. I would like to hear you say something good about competition.

Nagler: I could probably say something better about competition than a Buddhist could any day! [*laughter*] Seriously, I am not well trained in Buddhism, but from my understanding there is no such thing as duality in the absolute world. But we live in the relative world. And it is in the relative world where our responsibility functions—having to decide, sometimes quite dualistically, between things which are good and things which are bad, in the sense that they will bring us either to a good end or a disastrous end. There is a documentary on Sri Easwaran that we had made in 1980 in which he described that moment in his spiritual development when the barrier fell between the inner world and the outer world, and he said from that point on the inner world was as real for him as the outer world. And he added, "The outer world *is real*." It never became unreal for him; but the inner world became as real for him. So there is an appropriate way to act within each of those realms. When we are acting in the phenomenal (or outer) world as individuated creatures, as the Buddha said, I believe, "Dharma is not to be clung to; how much the less adharma." We do have to make a distinction between dharma and adharma when we are functioning with our eyes open as conscious creatures (or congratulating ourselves that we are so doing!).

I understand that this question came up recently at a talk given by Tenzin Palmo, the Buddhist nun of Tibetan lineage who is now giving dharma talks after her rather dramatic twelve-year Himalayan retreat. Someone challenged her statement that we always need carefully to convert negative thoughts to positive thoughts on the grounds that it was dualistic, and she replied, "I'm very sorry; we are at the mercy of our emotions." So in the relative world we have to take responsibility for them.

But I'm sorry, you asked about competition. My teacher always held that even the competitive instinct was given to us for a reason. Everything was. We have rather taken the bit in our teeth here in America and made ourselves positively ill with our competitiveness, but it did originally have a creative purpose: to compete against ourselves! Was I pretty patient yesterday? Just watch my speed today. Like that.

Question: Actually, I was wondering if you could say something good about competition and conflict?

Nagler: In the field of peace studies today and conflict resolution we never say conflict is bad and that we are trying to get rid of it. But as a devotee of principled nonviolence I would add a theoretical ground for that point: that in the ultimate analysis there is no such thing as an irresolvable conflict. All conflict is conflict of perception. So we do not want the conflict to go away, but we want it to be resolved by peaceful means. We have the faith that there is no

reason for human beings to be in *divisive* conflict;
that all conflict is the signal of a learning opportunity.
In that framework, conflict has its place. Conflict is
unavoidable. There is a statement by an Air Force
general in a book that was widely read in the 1980s,
that "the one thing American people cannot deal with
is conflict." Implicit in this statement is the reason why
we need to have a military elite, and also why 70
percent of our GNP has to go down that drain: because
Americans will not take the responsibility to deal
with conflict. And the reason we cannot deal with it is
because we cannot deal with it in a nonviolent way;
everything has to set us up to be a winner or a loser.
The mass media in fact constantly present all human
interactions as win/lose conflict. For example, in the
recent California election, if you scan the papers you
will not find one mention of anyone's policy. The whole
discussion was about whether one person's career was
ruined, or, whether the other person's ego was gratified
because he had always wanted to be governor, and so
on. Everybody is looked at as a separate ego. In that
framework, conflict is terrifying. We can't solve it, so
we have to hire people to solve it for us. In principled
nonviolence, or even in creative conflict resolution as it
is best understood today, this threatening aspect of
conflict is removed and we can set about dealing with
it creatively.

Question: How does such a philosophy as
yours prevail? How does it increase its followers and
adherents? I mean, how effective really is the tailgate

approach to the kind of transformation you wish to see come about? Is it not inspired and brought about by individuals? Yet you just seemed to locate the problem of violence and conflict as centered on individualism, the separate ego?

Nagler: I see that I've caused a problem by using the term "individual." By this I certainly did not mean the narcissistic, private, sometimes known as "rugged" individual who is indeed the cause of all violence, but rather the *participatory* individual fully alive to his or her being-in-the-world. As another writer said recently, this is precisely "a matter of shifting the center of consciousness from the small egocentric self, with its desires and aversions, to the vast all-inclusive self [or Self], from the appearance to the Reality."[32] And here's Gandhi: "The purpose of life is undoubtedly to know oneself. We cannot do it unless we learn to identify ourselves with all that lives." In other words, he's saying, in his inimitable manner, that our real self is the Self, the ground of "all that lives." (He goes on to say, incidentally, "The sum total of that life is God. Hence the necessity of realizing God living within every one of us. The instrument of this knowledge is boundless selfless service.") Perhaps I should have said the person instead of the individual.

To back up a bit, in the new paradigm generally, and particularly with regard to its view of living systems, the relationship of "part" to "whole" is different from that held in the prevailing view. Each "part" (the word is not ideal for the new concept) has a "holographic" relationship to the whole: Gandhi was fond of quoting a Sanskrit proverb, which roughly translates "whatever is in the microcosm is in the macrocosm."[33] This has enormous consequences for violence/nonviolence, as I've tried to show elsewhere.[34] In any case, this is the kind of "individual" I was referring to: not the part, conceivably separate from the whole, but more like a *locus* of reality which (or rather, who) needs to be recovered today as a recovery from dehumanization.

The paradox is not going to go away (at least until the new paradigm comes), but it is often invoked: as Martin Luther King did when he famously said, "I can never be what I ought to be until you are what you ought to be. You can never be what you ought to be until I am what I ought to be." My fulfillment cannot be purchased at the expense of yours—that is essential to all nonviolence; indeed, we can go further: my fulfillment only comes when I am wholeheartedly striving for yours. As the Buddha said, in the final sense, my fulfillment depends on yours, on everyone's.

Now dehumanization, which for me is the core of all violence, is first and foremost the devaluing and finally the obliteration of the person, in favor of— well, of anything else. It was a sad day when that circuit judge somewhere in the South decided that corporations have rights! But the only way to recover the reality of the person, as everyone from Aristotle to Hillary Clinton has recognized, is in *community*.

The beloved community is the community of empowered individuals, *but* to the degree that we let even a community raise itself *above* the individual, we are sliding away from love and back into a stage-two regime of unanimous violence.

Gandhi developed the simple world-order model of the "oceanic circle" to show how we could articulate the fully alive, "rediscovered" individual with the whole world order. On the other hand, the greedy, obsessed, autistic individual will not be able to participate in this vibrant whole and—our paradox again—ceases being a real individual to that extent. As Meister Eckhart said, "The zero, placed in front of the One, that is, of God, has no value; placed after the One it gains great value."

Your question was also, how would such a sweeping change happen if I see it arising from individuals. Well, that's your old paradigm shift again, which is still unpredictable; but the one thing that *is* predictable is that when the ingredients are in the right place at the right time, it happens. I mentioned the work of Ray and Anderson on Cultural Creatives; there is also *The Tipping Point* by Malcolm Gladwell, which can be applied, though his scope is somewhat more modest, to this new science of "chaotic" change.[35] Let me add from my own point of view as a nonviolence scholar that one of the faith positions in principled nonviolence is that when you have empowered individuals you do not need to worry about the numbers; the numbers will take care of themselves. This is an aspect of the principle known as *svadeshi*.

I have roughly translated it as "local concern": we may be familiar with its economic application, where it translated into self-reliance, cottage industry— the boycott of foreign goods. Like most of Gandhi's operational terms, however, it had deeper dimensions, and it could be even applied to the limitless nature of the inner power of the person (and the dynamic which states that if you take care of that power even in the most limited circle, the circumference of that circle expands).

Of course it is not limited to India. Epictetus, again, said, "The only thing you can control, and therefore the only thing you need to control, is the imagery in your own mind." So if you break contact with the mass media as an individual, and start taking some responsible control through prayer, meditation, and similar practices of the images in your own mind, you begin to influence other people. The more cleanly you do that core job, the more widely the circle can expand. It is important to emphasize this point, because with our external orientation we worry unduly, I think, about numbers and organizations and not enough about the *quality* of the mind within. Gandhi, Thoreau, and all devotees of principled nonviolence were concerned to correct this emphasis. I like to think it's not what kind of people we put in power that really counts, but what kind of power we put in people.

Question: I understood you to imply that changing the emphasis from matter to consciousness will lead to nonviolence?

Nagler: Yes, it should. But the question I am asking myself is why hasn't it? In other words, physicists have made this tremendous breakthrough, just a century old now, to see that consciousness underlies all experience. As Planck said, "Consciousness I regard as fundamental. I regard matter as derivative from consciousness . . . everything that we regard as existing postulates consciousness." Yet there is no way for this groundbreaking, tremendous insight to make it through the filters of the prevailing paradigm, rigidly maintained by popular culture.

Question: . . . but what is to prevent one from saying, "My consciousness is better than your consciousness," or what's to prevent that consciousness from getting translated into ideas of God, religion, and the kind of thinking that leads to religious wars and violence?

Nagler: Oh. I was talking about an ontology, or a faith, if you will, in consciousness as a supreme principle; not "my consciousness" versus anyone else's. In other words, I was not referring to competing miniscule fragments of consciousness, filtered through so many veils of conditioning. So in speaking of prioritizing consciousness over matter, I was really speaking of a process whereby we would rehumanize ourselves, because we would stop thinking of ourselves as a machines, that is, as matter. We are spirit disguised as matter, and I was talking about dropping the disguise—or not taking it for the person.

Nonetheless, your question is very important, and always comes up when we're discussing—not consciousness, perhaps, but truth: If I am to cling to the truth as I see it, and if it's inevitable that your truth and mine will differ, what is to prevent us from fighting and/or trying to dominate each other? Gandhi dealt with this most famously in his response to that very question at a commission hearing. He said, the individual must indeed be the final witness to his or her truth, but that was perfectly all right as long as he or she would also adopt nonviolence. Then the more opinions differ, the merrier: it would all be part of the search for truth in which we must always be engaged to be fully alive, fully human. I would add another criterion which Gandhi also espoused: since we are limited, after all, and none of us can see the absolute truth (as Faust said, ours is the striving after truth, truth itself can only be known by God), we should always hold our beliefs, however much we cherish them, as hypotheses. We should always be ready to drop or modify them if they confront better insight. Einstein was famous for this.

Question: Is the individual opposed to the community, or is the solution to universalize consciousness, to go from small individual identity to the Hindu conception of "universal consciousness" because this consciousness *is* the one that relieves violence, because I am confident that's part of myself?

Nagler: Yes, I did not mean to imply that I was opposed to the community. "Community" is a very positive word, but I used it in a negative sense here, and probably what I really meant was the "collective"—*Gesellschaft*. My problem was that in the ancient world there isn't a nation-state, so we need some general term for the political "container" of social life (as my colleague Manfred Steger says). In recent times it became the "Westphalian" nation-state, and today there is no question that the biggest threat to our humanity is the corporation. As none other than Mussolini said, fascism may as well be called corporatism; and Hannah Arendt will add, as we've seen, that fascism (corporatism) "strives not toward despotic rule over men but toward a system in which men [and women] are superfluous." My point is that none of these abstractions should ever be given priority, should ever have the right of life and death over the individual, because after all is said and done, no collective is sentient, alive. The collective does not exist except insofar as conscious beings decide to act as if it did.

I was also making the point, or leading up to it, that in the modern age, the best if not the only way to find fulfillment by discovering God, the source of all consciousness, is within us. Do that and no advertisement will ever bother you again! But I

certainly did not mean to imply that when you have
realized the supreme consciousness by going within
yourself (I'm calling this modern, but that's how
Heraclitus did it!) you discover that it's *only* within
yourself, because you simultaneously discover that
your real Self is not limited to the body or any
"component thing" that we call the person. On the
contrary, it's everywhere. So genuine realization, in my
view, is in fact the ultimate community. I was saying
only that the Self, if I may use that Hindu construct,
is everywhere, but "within" is the efficient place to look
for it. As William Law said, "Though God be
everywhere present, yet He is only present to thee in
the deepest and most central part of thy soul."[36]

Question: Could you comment on the issue of
vegetarianism? How important is that to nonviolence
in your opinion?

Nagler: Intuitively it is quite important. It was of
fundamental importance to Gandhi; his family had
been vegetarian for centuries. In Bihar when he was
working on the Champeran issue in 1917, he was
joined by many people from all over India and some of
them were not vegetarians. So, the question arose how
they might work this out. Gandhi suggested two
separate kitchens: one for the vegetarians, and another
for nonvegetarians. One week later the nonvegetarians
folded up their kitchen, came over and said, "Can we
eat with you?" So, I think there is a natural resonance,

on more than one level, between vegetarianism and nonviolence. First of all, there is the obvious one of *ahimsa*, you do not want to do harm to living creatures who are conscious enough to be aware of that harm. But also, it seems that if you look at the various ramifications of vegetarianism, they all add up to the same norm from their different standpoints: vegetarianism is cheaper, better for one's health, environmentally sound, and after a while it tastes better . . . and there's a reason all of these cohere. The universe is telling us something: that this is the way for human beings to go. There was a thousand-year tradition of vegetarianism in the ancient world, which was squashed in the year 92 AD when one of the Roman emperors expelled philosophers from Rome. But who knows what would have happened if that tradition remained unbroken. I very much like the book by Keith Akers, *The Lost Religion of Jesus*, subtitled *Simple Living and Vegetarianism in Early Christianity*, in which he argues that not only was Jesus vegetarian, but he was belligerent about it to the point of being a militant vegetarian. This is why he kicked those people out of the temple, which had basically become an *abattoir* for sacrificial offerings at that time. Of course, one can say practically anything one wants about Jesus because there is not enough evidence to prove it or disprove it. But Akers's reconstruction seems very well founded to me.

The reason for my rather lengthy answer, for which I apologize, is that I do not want to say that any doctrine, even an obvious one like vegetarianism, is essential—that you cannot be nonviolent unless you are vegetarian. But I do say that if you adopt the principle of nonviolence in a growing way, it will naturally lead you there. You will reach a point where you feel that much more kinship and compassion with living beings, and thus you do not want to be involved in harming them. After all, the Buddha said, "Do not kill; and do not be *involved* in killing." Do not help others to kill. Eventually you will reach that point, but I think a person has to reach it in his or her own way.

Question: Do you think that physical contact helps to promote nonviolence? For example, hugs and embraces?

Nagler: I think it is essential for very young creatures; but then it is something that we have to slowly rise above. But again, this is an individual matter, and everyone needs to decide for him- or herself. Nonetheless, as Aristotle said, if you know you are heavily weighted over on the right, push far to the left, and you will end up in the center. We live in an environment which is heavily sensate; we are being told hundreds of times a day that it is only through physical contact with the product I want to sell you, or the person sitting next to you in your sports car, or whatever, that you will have communion and satisfaction. If we were smart, we would push ourselves a bit on the other side. My teacher insisted that the real way to achieve union between man and woman is through tenderness and respect. His style was never crude or strident; like "unhand me, you wretch!" or "no touching." He simply said that as you increase in tenderness and respect your reliance on physical contact would diminish. On the other hand, you may be involved in a relationship with someone who hasn't yet reached that point, and of course this would include a child; they may demand a certain amount of physical contact. The skill in that case would be, I imagine, to be able to have some physical contact, even enjoy it, but with detachment . . . I will let you know when I get there!

Question: Could you help us understand the distinction between what you call "the integral and sacred nature of self," and the "self" that is involved in the Enlightenment and the rise of science and technology?

Nagler: The word or concept of "self" is tricky, as we've seen. We exist in competing images of who we are. And when I use the word, therefore, I may be referring to something different than when you use the word. However, when I think about the rise of science and modern technology I like to use the aforementioned Upanishadic model that says, "Above the senses is the mind, above the mind is the intellect—discriminative awareness— above the intellect is ego, the individuating principle; and above that is what they call undifferentiated consciousness; and above that, finally, is the Supreme Reality, or Brahman." This puts intellect, and with it the achievements of modern science, in perspective, in a way of which Dante would have approved. Look at the university for example, which to its disgrace is struggling mightily to retain control over the national weapons labs: there you have, in my view, an excellent example of the limitations of intellect. That is intellect without wisdom; without any vision, or as Dr. A. T. Ariyaratne says, "scientific knowledge without the knowledge of righteousness."[37] That is what happens when the problem-solving capacity of the human being, which is indeed very impressive, tries to operate "without moral insight" as Oppenheimer echoes. Moral insight must involve our innate relationship with one another and a complete refusal to work harm to anyone as a solution to any problem. This is something that needs and deserves much more discussion. Swami Vivekananda said just a hundred years ago that our besetting difficulty here in the West is that we cultivate the intellect and neglect the heart, that this would only make us ten times greedier, and eventually this would be the ruin of us. That doesn't look far wrong today!

Thank you; your questions helped me improve my thinking on these issues, surely among the most important issues for our time, and I hope that you may also have enjoyed and benefited from the interchange as much as I have.

Epilogue

PROFESSOR MUDGE HAS CHALLENGED ME, or asked me, to apply the vision of modern culture that I outlined above—by attempting to juxtapose it to the universal wisdom tradition—to "those millions of people who sit Sunday mornings in pews." As he put it, "How do we get under their skins?"

If anyone doubted the pertinence of this question, it has become dramatically more obvious with the national election results of November 2 last year. That election was influenced, perhaps decisively, by Evangelical Christian voters who regarded President Bush (to my mind, quite irrationally) as the more "religious" of the two contenders for the position of the most politically powerful single individual on earth.[38] I am among those who regard this decision as not only the wrong candidate but the wrong criterion, and its weight in the election as the sign of a catastrophic failure of political culture—*and* of those deeper levels of culture on which the political rests. Those who, like many in Europe, regarded the first George W. Bush administration as an American nightmare from which we, and the world, would awaken on November 2, 2004, must now come to grips with the fact that "religion," however understood, has become a pivotal factor in American politics, and that this can be a factor that throws its weight on the wrong side of the scale. "Religion," as it seems to me, is becoming a force that diametrically opposes the original core values of the major faiths, not only

Christianity but all human culture. Religious "conservatives" (an oddly misleading designation) do things in the name of Jesus to which he was flatly opposed—which indeed he died to overcome.

Bill Moyers recently referred to this phenomenon as "the delusional coming in from the margins of discourse and being now central."[39] According to a 2002 *Time*/CNN poll, he reports, 59 percent of Americans believe that the prophecies found in the book of Revelation are going to come true. In my terms, if such a trend gains ground it will push Christianity two thousand years backwards to a pagan, stage-two religion based on fantastic—and extremely violent—mythologies. It is extremely significant in this connection that "Christian Zionists" (they are neither) predict and seek the rebuilding of the temple in Jerusalem *and what it stood for*: a priesthood and animal sacrifices instead of Jesus's self-sacrifice for the redemption of mankind.[40] A more explicit reversion to paganism could not be imagined, as anyone familiar with the works of René Girard will recognize.

Unfortunately, this form of religious delusion resonates with (and supports) a not dissimilar retreat from reality in contemporary politics. When writer Ron Suskind was talking recently with a presidential adviser, the latter said that Suskind was:

> . . . "in what we call [dismissively] the reality-based community," . . . who "believe that solutions emerge from your judicious study of discernible reality." I nodded and murmured

something about enlightenment principles and empiricism. He cut me off. "That's not the way the world really works anymore. . . . We're an empire now, and when we act we create our own reality."[41]

In the immortal words of Josef Stalin, "We ourselves will be able to determine what is true and what is not."[42] This is a terrifying mentality to have installed itself in the high seats of office of any country. As the Mahabharata puts it, "Delusion leads to death."[43]

I take this opportunity, therefore, to respond somewhat more fully to Professor Mudge's pertinent challenge. At the same time, I broaden it to include what we can do to get under the skins of people who do not frequent those parish pews. Churches are certainly a privileged and important venue, but not the only one in which the new dialogue has to take place if we are to put delusion back in its place on the remotest fringes of social discourse.

Before I begin to tackle this question, how we can begin to restore this potentially catastrophic loss of human understanding, I want to respond again to the question that was posed earlier: how can we have faith in the personalistic approach I outlined (in the footsteps of Mother Teresa), which seems so small in scale to be opposed to such a Goliath of a problem? I would remind us of what so many teachers of humanity have recalled to us—that there is a world within, never stained, ever untouched by the play of delusion outside us. Our job is not to succeed (though that's also nice) but to do what we can, as Merton pointed out—so that God can make something out of it. Like it or not, it is ours to work in the spirit of a story that's told about a Buddhist monastery somewhere in Thailand. A student rushes in to report that somewhere nearby an entire teak forest has burned to the ground. "Take seedlings," the teacher calmly replies, "and start replanting."

"But it takes a thousand years to make a teak forest," says the student.

"Then we must begin at once," the teacher replies.

This is why I measured our modern civilization against the accumulated wisdom of our human ancestors, in the talk above. I know it has been a rather painful exercise. Almost a cheap shot—but one I feel that had to be fired. We need to know what the forest looks like even if we may never, in this lifetime, walk its cool shadows and enjoy the life teeming from floor to canopy within it.

Let us begin by putting the misuse of Christianity Moyers and others have drawn attention to in a historical framework. All religions seem to pass through three stages, often repeating them in cycles. There is the original *revelation* of the religion's founding figure, usually one of the great avatars such as Jesus, Mohammed, or Buddha. The inspiration of this explosive discovery, while it helps make a decisive break with institutions the receiving community has outgrown, is too great a challenge for the ordinary mortal to live up to, certainly in practice and usually also in belief. In its pure form the founder's vision can endure as a serious call to the devout for only a few decades, conceivably a few centuries in a favorable culture (the deserts of upper Egypt, for example), and then there follows, as there must, a period of *accommodation.* Augustine is a good example of a spiritual genius who knew that if the Christian system was to prevail among the masses it would have to be watered down (and Christianity was well served, actually, by his being able to do so with such compassionate intelligence). But in time, as the second law of thermodynamics states, all things wind down. Once launched, accommodation continues to dilute the original revelation until it is nearly gone; as they say in India, a religion is like a path through the jungle: if no one walks on it for a while it becomes overgrown. At this point there is nothing left of the religion—except, dangerously enough, its prestige. The final stage is *cooptation*: at this point "religion" can be invoked for anything, for the reinstatement of those very institutions, practices, and beliefs it came into being to supplant. For example, with regard to violence, leaders begin to realize that the safest way to keep any interdiction against violence posed by their religion from actually inhibiting violence is to make the religion itself its cause. Those who manipulate power cannot resist the temptation of this great source of legitimacy, now evacuated of content; in their hands the religion now becomes a dangerous force, a claim on emotions that are lower than reason, not an appeal to insights that transcend it. This is the stage that we have now reached, as Bill Moyers, Jim Wallis, and many other alarmed commentators have noted.

The political results of our allowing the mainstream religion of the country to go so long without a renewal, a regrounding in its basic principles, are now clear.[44] Not to put too fine a point on it, America is moving into a totalitarian condition not too different from fascism. I do not use the term lightly. In a sermon delivered by Rev. Davidson Loehr on November 7, 2004 at the First Unitarian Universalist Church of Austin, Rev. Loehr, in the footsteps of Umberto Eco (who had suffered directly under fascism properly so called), outlined fifteen characteristics of that kind of regime. I am afraid we exhibit all of them now, including the most abominable.[45] But the mistakes that got us here are not only political; Aldous Huxley predicted long ago that materialism would end up putting us in this authoritarian straightjacket. And the opposite of materialism, spirituality, will get us out. This is why the role of religion in these recent developments has been so disheartening.

Christianity is by no means the only religion to go through this devolutionary cycle, or to be in the bottom stage of it right now, but it is Christianity we must be mostly concerned with in this country. And while this cycle seems to be well-nigh universal there are some special characteristics of Christianity (or rather, of the Western tradition), which may help us understand its own vulnerability to cooptation.

It has always seemed to me that the divorce between religion and science was one of the greatest setbacks to Western civilization. For religion it meant a descent into dogmatism, because it would deprive religion from grounding in the only kind of reality that would eventually come to matter in the West. But science also has not fared all that well. For science the plunge was into a dusty reductionism made to seem very exciting for a while by glittering technological advances, but ultimately most demoralizing. As Alvin Toffler said, the notion that the universe was mechanical and its movements inescapably determined "aroused enthusiasm. But it also came as a shock that nature described in this way was . . . debased: by the very success of science, nature was shown to be an automaton, a robot" and every new breakthrough "ends upon a tragic note. This very progress . . . makes us gypsies of the universe."[46] Science became, as we've seen, an attempt to explain all reality as the dance of inert, material objects—a thing which never was and never can be.[47] Fortunately.

This divorce of the religion from science is almost unique to Christianity, arising from certain dynamics of the European Renaissance. Perhaps the proximity of once widely different faith traditions to one another in this shrinking world (I recently spoke on peace in a local synagogue where Buddhism was being discussed in the adjoining room) the mighty task of reconciling these two great projects, science and religion, empiricism and faith, may not be as difficult as once seemed. Who knows? With everything else up for grabs in this chaotic world perhaps it is time now for the "traditional" divorce to begin being reconciled. If so—if it is done so as to combine the best of each, not to subject one framework to the other—it would remove a road block that has stymied the forward thrust to a new paradigm that we so badly need. There is no harm thinking big at this point in time; indeed, there may be no other way to save ourselves. Just as I have tried to include the political dimension in a talk on spirituality, I feel that we have to begin thinking about such sweeping changes as a redefinition of faith and empiricism that would get them both at least roughly on the same page. The unavoidable connection among all these formerly isolated dots is really part of what the new paradigm, the new message is all about. The prevailing paradigm sees them in isolation. We cannot afford to.

While we desperately need to move forward, it will be difficult to manage a Kierkegaardian leap into the unknown. That is one of the reasons a remarriage between religion and science would be so helpful. Imagine the explanatory power of an inquiring system that included both perspectives, the best insights of both modes of knowing! It would make the reconciliation of relativity and quantum theory insignificant by comparison. Mind you, I do not have a clear sense of how to broker the remarriage: what is clear, however, is that spirituality would renew religion, reground science—and rescue politics.

Here, too, the greater accessibility of the world's great faith traditions to one another could be of immense significance, for in most of them there is less distance already between religion and science. So we see again that the great discoveries of all religions could be, and perhaps were always meant to be, mutually supportive. As my teacher used to say, to get a full view of the Himalayas you need to see them from India, Pakistan, Nepal, and China—each has something to contribute.

The first time I read *Hind Swaraj*, Gandhi's famous critique of modern civilization, it seemed like a welcome confirmation of everything I believed in, until I reached the Mahatma's pronouncement that any nation that wants to realize its destiny "cannot afford to despise its ancestors."[48] I was, after all, typically Western in many ways and it was the late sixties. We were inventing the world in those days, and had little patience for the findings of anyone from the pre-psychedelic age. I am wiser now—at least in this respect. Experience has shown me, too, that we cannot afford to overlook wisdom anywhere, and particularly in our own tradition, where it is most accessible to us and least liable to cross-cultural misunderstandings. In this sense we must drop back, as the French say, for a better spring forward. At the same time, I have made bold to modify Gandhi's advice, and I believe the Mahatma would approve. He was talking about recovering India's ancient spiritually-rooted civilization, which I agree is one of the wonders of the world, while I have been talking about recovering that *plus* the many echoes of the sane wisdom in other civilizations;

in a word, the wisdom tradition as a whole—that marvelous body of insight into reality which we ignore to our peril, which any human being can now claim with ever greater plausibility as the world shrinks. Globalization has been a curse because it has been in the hands of centralized authorities who are, almost by vocation, addicted to the greed for wealth and power. We can turn it into a blessing if we take this opportunity—as some of us already are—to make our own the wisdom of *all* our forebears, which is to arrive in the twenty-first century, as Einstein said, remembering our humanity before all else.

What would be the biggest single question we would wish to solve, with that great resource? "For our culture as a whole," Huston Smith recently pointed out, "nothing major is going to happen until we figure out who we are. The truth of the matter is, that today we haven't a clue as to who we are. There is no consistent view of human nature in the West today."[49] How could there be? I recently saw a bumper sticker that said, "We Are Spiritual Beings Having a Physical Experience." We are spirit, masquerading as, or temporarily dwelling in, bodies, as all wisdom has told us since it began being recorded. But we find ourselves in a bleak thought-world of materialism, partly of our own devising. In such a world, how can we figure out who we are when the only possibility that happens to be true is ruled out? And so the project on which we must embark, churchgoers or pagans, is to *recover a sense of humanity—of Who We Are—through an awakening of spiritual culture.*

It is said often, and rightly, that we are experiencing a "Promethean" crisis. We are being swept aside as conscious agents by a runaway technology, which no one seems able to control, which has taken on a life of its own. We are seeing what Aldous Huxley predicted, alas all too prophetically, "the abolition of free will by methodical conditioning,"[50] all driven by the relentless emphasis on thingness, materiality, of the world of objects until we ourselves become such objects—in our depleted imaginations. As my teacher used to say, "Greed for profits and blind faith in technology are causing us to forfeit the well-being of our children" and everything that makes human life worth living. In an earlier decade the most prominent form of the Promethean crisis was the nuclear threat, which is still there and certainly dangerous enough, but I have pointed to the technology of communication systems, of the mass media. They have given rise to a highly uniform popular culture that has not only driven alternatives off the field in the industrialized West but in unsuspecting societies around the globe, often with even worse results for those societies than for ours. Progressives have drawn attention, rightly, to the political bias of the general mainstream media, but the media are wrecking democracy in at least two other ways. These are the words of Dante Zappala, whose brother died in Iraq looking for weapons that were not there—that were known to be not there. He is commenting on all of us: "We shut down our ability to think critically, to listen, to converse and to act. We are to blame."[51] How did we get so "dumbed down?" How did we become a nation that would rather feel good than think, even to save itself? Can there be any doubt that the endless barrage of commercial messages has done that?

But the damage runs even deeper, into what we might call the ontological bankruptcy of materialism itself. I have emphasized one aspect of this ontology, namely *dehumanization*. By investing so much of our attention on the lifeless world, we come finally to believe that we ourselves are without life or consciousness—machines, without human meaning. I imagine that this delusion happened in stages. First, simple tools were devised to help alleviate human labor, and who could quarrel with it: man was not meant to labor in the fields all day for bare subsistence, as so many still do. Then, however, machines were invented to *replace* human labor, which is problematic. And the next step was more so: machines invented to assist communication, similarly, ended up *replacing* human communication—why go down the hall to talk to someone when you can get them on the phone or send an email? And now we have a world where, as Mr. Winston's people proudly boast, you can have a "meaningful relationship" with a robot—because, let's face it, you think you're nothing but a machine yourself. *I, Robot* is the exciting name of a film that's going around, and the creepy posters for it tell how far we've fallen from awareness of our human nature. People are weirdly thrilled to think of themselves as not-people. I recently received an ad for my very own toy robot, modeled on aerospace designs, called "Robosapiens." Sixty-nine moves, mind you, for only a hundred bucks or so. A small price to pay for forgetting that I am alive, conscious, and responsible!

This dehumanization is probably the greatest falsehood about human nature ever perpetrated, and the cost of it in alienation, despair, and violence has been enormous. While I have emphasized the commercial role of the mass media in creating a dehumanized worldview, I also had to point out that the kind of "science" that the mass media feed to unsuspecting consumers has the same dehumanizing effect. This is what I tried to show with the clever—albeit unconscious—filtering of the article on nicotine addiction cited above, and examples could be multiplied: in a more recent article on Post-Traumatic Stress Disorder (PTSD) the writer (a scientist, not a journalist) defines the condition as "a debilitating, sometimes lifelong *change in brain chemistry* that can include flashbacks, sleep disorders, panic attacks . . . and emotional numbness."[52]

Now, all this comes just at the time, as mentioned above, when real science is allowing itself some rather eye-opening breakthroughs into the spiritual nature of reality. It would require a separate book to review these developments, and some have been written, but I would like to mention some avenues that seem particularly relevant. *Forgiveness* has received a good bit of attention in science, establishing it along with faith as what the late Norman Cousins called a "therapeutic reality." Similarly *empathy*. Sophisticated noninvasive techniques for registering brain activity have led to the discovery of "shadow neurons," mimetic responses of one person's central nervous system to the emotions and behavior of another— watching someone cry evokes a crying response in me, which may or may not stop short of tears. Similarly with *altruism*: Gregory S. Berns, neuroscientist at Emory University, has shown that altruistic moves, even in a game setting such as Prisoners' Dilemma, evoke in one who makes them the kind of brain activity witnessed during drug highs or other "intensely pleasurable experiences."[53] And for the other side of that coin, scientists, military historians, and others have been uncovering the fact long known in various ways to military planners and soldiers themselves, that there is a built-in inhibition against killing or injuring another widely present in humans (how and wherever we imagine that the building-in resides). Peace psychologist Rachel MacNair has coined the term Perpetration Induced Traumatic Stress (PITS, appropriately) for the fact that soldiers who kill suffer untold mental or spiritual damage that is often harder to bear than any physical injuries they themselves endured.[54] This problem is already assuming alarming proportions with the invasion of Iraq, and the Army has no way to deal with it. As retired Army psychiatrist Colonel Holloway explains, the Army does not talk about this widespread phenomenon because to do so "would pathologize an absolutely necessary experience."[55] But PITS (also known as human empathy), which is a scandal to the old paradigm, an abomination to the military, is for us a bright glimpse of the hope that human nature is redeemable. They may shunt it aside but we should seize on it for confirmation that there is "that of God in every man" and woman, as the Quakers say, which cannot be denied and which instead we should enthusiastically develop.

How? Let me first talk about a problem I do *not* know how to solve, but which must be solved at some point in this process of recovery. Anyone who has watched those modern television versions of India's ancient epics (with or without subtitles), must be struck by one thing: how gems of spiritual wisdom were craftily embedded thousands of years ago in narratives that can today be reproduced in, frankly, somewhat childish "action movies" that can hold the attention of the least sophisticated viewer. India, for all its problems, somehow managed to embed a certain amount of wisdom in pop culture, and I have no idea how we would reproduce that. One shudders to think of Mel Gibson as our answer to the Mahabharata!

But I have shared a few ideas about other ways to unblock the needed paradigm shift. I listed five things that can be done by anyone to get him- or herself out of the prevailing delusion of materialism, separateness, and violence and I did this in the confidence that such a person becomes a locus of restorative energy for others and, in time, the system as a whole. I made no excuses for starting small not only because it's so doable—small is probably the only place to start—but because since the world within can only be reached through oneself, it is the best place. Let me now revisit that list with special attention to church people and the churchgoing audiences as per Professor Mudge's challenge.

1. First of all, there is a movement called "every church a peace church," and I for one, as an outsider, do not see how any Christian denomination worthy of the name can ignore the obvious nonviolent character of Jesus's message. The rediscovery of that glaring fact—the elephant in the room of Christianity, so to speak—has occurred cyclically throughout Christian history, as a fascinating little book by Quaker historian Geoffrey Nuttall shows, and we are ripe for another one.[56] I say this not only because I feel that there is an enormous potential of a renewed peace witness to renew the church itself in these awful times, because the very rationalism of these times has given us not only the support of behavioral sciences just mentioned but also, a new historical outlook that is less encumbered by traditional dogmatism. Whatever one may think about the latest wave of "historical Jesus" scholarship—and I know it is wallowing in controversy, where

it's not ignored—it does seem to me to establish two things about Jesus if anything can be established about his actual, historical person: (1) He was Jewish, and the Jewish people revered him. (This means that "the Jews" did not execute him; *some* Jewish elites likely had a hand in it along with the Roman occupation authorities.) And (2) he was nonviolent. I can almost hear the hornets I've stirred up here, so let me back away from this contentious area. But it does seem to me that peace is the one issue churches can teach and advocate as part of their core mission, without descending inappropriately into politics. We do not have to tell them how to vote, after all: we only have to remind them how to think.

2. As mentioned above, even fairly conservative mainline churches should find a way to offer their parishioners at least a taste of that "reverent study" of other religions Gandhi refers to—and be it noted that "reverent" in this connection means an appreciation of the inner sameness of all faiths, not a harping on their superficial differences.

3. Now for a fundamental point: churches are in a good position to expose the relentless lie that we are inert machines rucking about in a meaningless universe, or maybe animals pushed

and pulled by molecules, hormones, programmed by genes—in a word, helpless, and therefore blissfully irresponsible. No institution is better positioned to insist that we are spirit disguised as body—and longing to recover our real identity.

One way to do this, it seems to me, would be simply to refute the lie when it comes up. Almost at random, I cite one story told in my local paper by a volunteer who was helping with relief work after the December 26, 2004, tsunami in South Asia. This volunteer kept stressing, "I'm alive, they're not." The whole emphasis was on herself, on separation— even in that selfless context when human beings usually rise to some awareness of our interconnectedness, what Thich Nhat Hanh would call our "interbeing." If I had been asked to give a sermon the next Sunday I would have insisted, "No, you've got it wrong, the point of the tragedy is not its stark separation of the dead from the living. A part of us died with them, a part of them lives in us."

4. What I have to say now should really be number one. It all has to begin with the personal cultivation of mind through meditation and prayer. Recently *U.S. News and World Report* published a list of fifty things everyone

can do to improve their life, and they listed "learn to meditate" as number two on that list. Perhaps, with that endorsement, I no longer need to be apologetic about this appeal! Yet, ironically, as we all know, it may run into more difficulties in the nation's churches than it does in *Business Week* and the *U.S. News.* Where that difficulty arises (and it is by no means true of all congregations) it comes mostly from thinking of meditation as an Eastern practice, a misconception that partly results from the mere terminological fact that when meditation was practiced in the Western church (here I include Syriac and Orthodox writings) it was often called "interior prayer," "prayer of silence" or the like. It is time for the West to rediscover meditation— if not now, when? If not in churches, where? By turning away from the splendid lineage even here in the Roman West from Augustine to Francis to Meister Eckhart to Saint Teresa to near-contemporary Thérèse of Lisieux, are we not breaking contact with our ancestors in the crippling way that Gandhi pointed out?

5. Let me end where I began, with nonviolence. I mentioned that some churches are already studying books provided by the Blue Mountain Center (and some are using my own book, *Search for a Nonviolent Future,* as well).

Recently Chris Hedges, the journalist who wrote *War is a Force That Gives Us Meaning,* was interviewed by the magazine *Yes!* Quoting his conclusion in the book that "lurking beneath the surface of every society . . . is the passionate yearning for a nationalist cause . . . that war alone is able to deliver," the interviewer asked if he thus thought that war is inevitable. He replied, "The only force that is powerful enough to subvert the force of war is love. Love is never organized. Love is always individual. . . . In wartime, everything is done to subvert that force."[57] A nearly perfect statement. When he calls love an individual force he is lined up with everything I've been saying about the discovery of the person, likewise when he says in the same vein that war is in essence dehumanization, that "there are times when remaining human is the only resistance possible." But in one respect I beg to differ. Love, while individual in origin, in essence, can indeed be organized. What else is nonviolence?

Notes

1. If email accounts are to be trusted, this was none other than Osama Bin Laden's personal physician.

2. "The Fourth R," *Journal of the National Institute of Dispute Resolution* 74 (August–September 1996): 1.

3. *Santa Rosa Press Democrat*, November 5, 2004.

4. For example, Natalie Angier, "Why We're So Nice: We're Wired to Cooperate," *New York Times*, July 23, 2002.

5. H. Stapp, "Quantum Physics and Human Values," Lawrence Berkeley Laboratory paper LBL-27738, September 2, 1989, 8–9.

6. Eknath Easwaran, *The Upanishads* (Tomales, CA: Nilgiri Press, 1995), 89. This is I.iii.10f in the Katha Upanishad.

7. Cited by Patrick Reinsborough, "How to Change Things," in *Globalize Liberation: How to Uproot the System and Build a Better World*, edited by David Solnit (San Francisco: City Lights Books, 2004), 172.

8. From a lecture given in July 1985. For a similar version see Easwaran, *The Upanishads*, 48.

9. Narayan Chaudhuri, *That Compassionate Touch of Ma Anandamayee* (Delhi: Motilal Benarsidass, 1998), 133.

10. Colin Tudge, "Enlightened Agriculture," *Resurgence* 221 (November/December 2003): 19. From his book *So Shall We Reap: What's Gone Wrong with the World's Food—and How to Fix It* (London: Penguin, 2003), 225–39.

11. Quoted in the film *The Day after Trinity*. See now on a development which may be even more dangerous, the following: "[Nanotechnologies] claim to be bringing within reach the Holy Grail sought by Western science since the days of Francis Bacon: the wielding of 'godlike' power and control over the basic forces of matter and energy." Lee-Anne Broadhead and Sean Howard, "The Heart of Darkness," *Resurgence* 221 (November/December 2003): 22.

12. *Confessions* 8.5 (my translation). It's the more remarkable that Augustine was able to make such a penetrating observation when you consider that a concept of the "will," in the modern sense, was relatively recent in Western philosophy. But then, mystics are remarkable.

13. John Saybrook, "It Came From Hollywood," *New Yorker*, December 1, 2003, 62.

14. Ibid. (emphasis added).

15. *The Washington Spectator* 29, no. 18 (October 1, 2003): 2 (quoting Madeleine Albright); originally in *Foreign Affairs* (September/October 2003).

16. *Iliad* 16.97–100 (emphasis added). My translation.

17. Simone Weil, *The Iliad, or The Poem of Force* (Wallingford, PA: Pendle Hill, 1956).

18. Michael N. Nagler, "Ethical Anxiety and Artistic Inconsistency: The Case of Oral Epic," in M. Griffith and D. J. Mastronarde, *Cabinet of the Muses* (Atlanta: Scholars Press, 1990), 225–39.

19. *City of God* 19.12 and Sadhu Vaswani quoted in *The Vision* 72, vol. 5 (February 2005): 189. Einstein, as another modern, added "and the whole of nature in its beauty" in a famous letter reprinted in the *New York Times* (March 29, 1972). The text is worth quoting in full:

> A human being is part of the whole, called by us "universe," a part limited in time and space. He experiences himself, his thoughts and feelings, as something separate from the rest—a kind of optical delusion of consciousness. This delusion is a kind of prison for us, restricting us to our personal desires and to affection for a few persons nearest to us. Our task must be to free ourselves from this prison by widening our circle of compassion to embrace all living creatures and the whole of nature in its beauty.

20. Christopher Lasch, *The Culture of Narcissism* (New York: Norton, 1979). Is it surprising that in the last four years cases of autism have doubled? Alongside the term "arrogant," the term most frequently occurring in descriptions of the president by psychologists is "narcissistic." In a culture of narcissism, narcissists seem like rulers.

21. Paul H. Ray and Sherry Ruth Anderson, *The Cultural Creatives: How 50 Million People Are Changing the World* (New York: Harmony Books, 2000).

22. It is notoriously difficult to do history on the life and meaning of Jesus, but my favorite reconstruction, as I will cite again later, is Keith Akers, *The Lost Religion of Jesus: Simple Living and Nonviolence in Early Christianity* (Lantern Books, 2000).

23. *Confessions* 5.1.4. This is the superb translation of Sr. Maria Boulding, O.S.B. (Hyde Park, NY: New City Press, 1997), 116.

24. Ed Sarath, "Meditation in Higher Education: The Next Wave?" *Innovative Higher Education* 27, no. 4 (Summer 2003).

25. *Collected Works of Mahatma Gandhi*, vol. 85, August 18, 1946. As a rough-and-ready description of the two practices today one often hears that prayer is speaking to God, while meditation is listening to God.

26. Michael N. Nagler, *The Search for a Nonviolent Future: A Promise of Peace for Ourselves, Our Families, and Our World* (Makawao, HI: Inner Ocean Publishing, 2002); www.mettacenter.org.

27. David F. Ford, *The Modern Theologians: An Introduction to Christian Theology in the Twentieth Century*, 2nd ed. (Oxford: Blackwell Publishers, 1997), 727.

28. Matthew Fox, *Original Blessing* (New York: Jeremy P. Tarcher/Putnam, 2000), 46.

29. *Ahimsa paramo dharma*, found repeatedly in the Mahabharata and other Sanskrit texts. Note that ahimsa is a more positive term than the literal translation "nonviolence" might imply (Nagler, *Search for a Nonviolent Future*, 44–45) and dharma is a profound concept that can also be translated "religion" (or nature, etc.).

30. The Gothic is *blodi-sijjian*. I have elsewhere commented that the Berrigans should have been aware of this when they sprinkled blood on draft files!

31. Mother Teresa, *Total Surrender* (New York: Walker, Missionaries of Charity, 1985), 123.

32. Eleanor Stark, *The Gift Unopened* (Boston: P. E. Randall, 1988), 123.

33. "yathā pinde, tathā brahmande" (as in the particle, so in the cosmic egg).

34. Michael N. Nagler, "Ideas of the World Order and the Map of Peace," in *Approaches to Peace: An Intellectual Map*, ed. W. Scott Thompson and Kenneth M. Jensen (Washington, D.C.: U.S. Institute of Peace, 1991), 371–92; see also chap. 9 of Nagler, *Search for a Nonviolent Future*.

35. Malcolm Gladwell, *The Tipping Point: How Little Things Can Make a Big Difference* (New York: Little, Brown, 2000).

36. Quoted in Eknath Easwaran, *God Makes the Rivers to Flow: Sacred Literature of the World Selected by Eknath Easwaran* (Tomales, CA: Nilgiri Press, 2003), 48.

37. Quoted in George D. Bond, *Buddhism at Work: Community Development, Social Empowerment and the Sarvodaya Movement* (Bloomfield, CT: Kumarian Press, 2004), 12.

38. A balanced account of their weight by Mark Danner concludes, "Still, having accounted, in their increased numbers, for a third of Bush's margin of victory, the evangelicals unquestionably form the Republican Party's most reliable and aggressive base of supporters. Their leaders have been quick and aggressive in claiming full credit for the triumph and the press has been happy to play along. As so often in politics, the appearance, through repetition, becomes its own reality." "How Bush Really Won," *New York Review of Books*, January 13, 2005.

39. On the occasion of Moyers receiving the Harvard Medical School Environment Citizen Award, on December 1, 2004. The text may be read at www.commondreams.org/views04/1206-10.htm.

40. Bill Durland, "Christian Zionism: Will Fear or Freedom Triumph?" *Friends Bulletin*, September 2004, 6.

41. Quoted by Anthony Grafton, "The Ways of Genius," *New York Review of Books*, December 2, 2004, 40.

42. Quoted by Anne Applebaum, "The Worst of the Terror," *New York Review of Books*, July 17, 2003, 17.

43. The full quote is, "Two destinies are established in this body, death and immortality. By choosing delusion one goes to death, by choosing renunciation, immortality."

44. Christianity is not really the dominant religion in America that it once was, as Diana Eck and others have shown. It is nonetheless perceived as such, and no doubt will be in the face of even more compelling evidence for some time to come.

45. The sermon may be read online: Davidson Loehr, "Living Under Fascism," November 7, 2004, http://www.uua.org/news/2004/voting/sermon_loehr.html. In *Sins of the Spirit, Blessings of the Flesh*, Matthew Fox makes the point that Hitler was able to appear as a man of religion because men of religion had failed to be truly of religion (New York: Three Rivers, 1999), app. A.

46. Alvin Toffler, introduction to Prigogine and Stengers, *Order Out of Chaos* (New York: Bantam, 1984), 3. The next quote is from p. 4.

47. As David Hawkins says, science, being linear, has become "progressively divorced from concern with the basis of life itself—[because] all life processes are, in fact, nonlinear." *Power vs. Force: The Hidden Determinants of Human Behavior* (Carlsbad, CA: Hay House, 2002), 42f.

48. *Hind Swaraj* or *Indian Home Rule* (Ahmedabad: Navajivan, 1938), 22. His actual words were, "A nation that is desirous of seeking home rule . . . ," but I belief this is a justified extension.

49. Quoted in Steven Glazer, *The Heart of Learning* (New York: Jeremy P. Tarcher/Putnam, 1999), 218.

50. Aldous Huxley, *Brave New World Revisited* (New York: Harper and Row, 1958), i.

51. *Los Angeles Times,* January 15, 2005.

52. *Santa Rosa Press Democrat,* November 15, 2004, A9.

53. Angier, "Why We're So Nice." The original study is James K. Rilling et al, "A Neural Basis for Social Cooperation," *Neuron* 35 (July 18, 2002): 395–405. (Needless to say, I do not believe that the biological corollary is the "basis" of the experience, but this is how scientists are prone to speak.)

54. Lt. Col. Dave Grossman, *On Killing: The Psychological Cost of Learning to Kill in War and Society* (Boston: Little, Brown, 1995).

55. Dan Baum, "The Price of Valor," *New Yorker,* July 12 and 19, 2004, http://www.newyorker.com/printables/fact/040712fa_fact.

56. Geoffrey Nuttall, *Christian Pacifism in History* (Berkeley and Chicago: World Without War, 1971).

57. *Yes!,* Winter 2005, pp. 20f. In the second ellipsis Hedges says, "Love is a force that is built between two human beings." Here, I believe, he is mistaken, and probably talking about the lower rungs of Plato's ladder of *eros* in *The Symposium.* Agapaic love is not so limited.

THE INSTITUTE
FOR WORLD RELIGIONS

With the understanding that spiritual values are central to the human experience, the Institute for World Religions exists to advance mutual understanding among the world's spiritual traditions. The Institute facilitates shared inquiry into the founding visions of the world's faiths so that all might learn from the others' strengths while preserving the integrity of their own.

The Institute for World Religions is also committed to providing an open forum where clergy, theologians, philosophers, scientists, educators, and individuals from a wide variety of disciplines can examine the role of religion in a modern world. All of the Institute's activities take place in an atmosphere of mutual respect and promote the universal human capacity for goodness and wisdom.

Established in 1976, the Institute was the direct result of the inspiration and planning of the Buddhist Chan Patriarch Hsüan Hua and Roman Catholic

Cardinal Yü Bin. Both of these distinguished international leaders in religion and education believed that harmony among the world's religions is an indispensable prerequisite for a just and peaceful world. Each shared the conviction that every religion should affirm humanity's common bonds and rise above narrow sectarian differences.

In keeping with its mission, the Institute offers programs designed to bring the major religious traditions together in discourse with each other and with the contemporary world. Its proximity to the University of California at Berkeley, Stanford University, the Graduate Theological Union, and the rich academic, religious, and cultural environment of the San Francisco Bay area provides an ideal environment for the Institute's programs.

The Institute publishes an annual journal, *Religion East and West,* in which some of *Our Spiritual Crisis* appeared in the June 2004 issue. *Religion East and West* furthers the Institute's mission of promoting knowledge about the world's religions through the medium of interfaith understanding and trust. It publishes articles by authors who are grounded in one or another of the great spiritual traditions, and who are immersed in the scholarly investigation of their own tradition and/or the traditions of others.

INDEX